Infinite Dendrogram

2. The Beasts of Undeath

Sakon Kaidou

Illustrator: **Taiki**

Hugo
Hugo Lesseps

A player Ray met in Gideon. He's notable for his pompous way of speaking and a disposition which doesn't allow him to ignore malignant deeds. Ray and Hugo team up to take care of a bandit group.

Ray
Ray Starling
Reiji Mukudori

A young man who — upon finishing his college entrance exams — began playing Infinite Dendrogram. Though generally a calm person, he has a strong will and sense of righteousness that allows him to keep struggling for as long as he needs to.

Nemesis
Nemesis

A girl that manifested as Ray's Embryo. She can change into weapons, and her first form allows her to become a greatsword. She also has quite an impressive appetite.

Cyco
Cyco

Hugo's partner, an excessively white girl. Currently busy both befriending and clashing with Nemesis — the excessively dark girl.

"Ray!"

I called out to him,
but he didn't answer.

"Forgive me!"

I poured the content of the
Potion into my mouth and
pushed my lips against his.

Infinite Dendrogram

2. The Beasts of Undeath

Sakon Kaidou

Illustrator: **Taiki**

Infinite Dendrogram: Volume 2
by Sakon Kaidou

Translated by Andrew Hodgson
Edited by Emily Sorensen

Copyright © 2017 Sakon Kaidou
Illustrations by Taiki

First published in Japan in 2017
Publication rights for this English edition arranged through Hobby Japan, Tokyo.

Find more books like this one at www.j-novel.club!

President and Publisher: Samuel Pinansky
Managing Editor: Aimee Zink

ISBN: 978-1-7183-5501-9
Printed in Korea
First Printing: September 2019
10 9 8 7 6 5 4 3 2 1

Contents

Kingdom of Altar, Cruella Mountain Belt

To the east of Gideon — the second largest city in the Kingdom of Altar — there was a mountainous area known as the Cruella Mountain Belt. It was the kingdom's border with Caldina — a country of expansive, desertlike wastelands.

For years, this border area had been a popular place for bandit gangs and their hideouts. Even if some group on a quest from the Adventurers' Guild eliminated one of them, they would soon be replaced by others.

There were two reasons for that.

The first was that the kingdom couldn't do any widescale and thorough bandit hunts due to the possibility of the neighboring country of Caldina seeing it as an act of war and thus provoking them.

The second was that the belt was on the primary trade route between Gideon, one of the kingdom's largest cities, and Caldina — a nation known for its mercantilism. A bandit couldn't ask for an area more plentiful with prey. Thus, the bandit problem in the belt was neverending.

However, it actually wasn't a bad thing for the Adventurers' Guild.

The new bandit gangs were always made up of people who went broke and got reduced to brigandry. Their jobs were low-rank and their levels weren't even maxed. Most active adventurers could eliminate them without much effort, and since it was a net positive for the adventurer economy, the guild wasn't averse to the idea of the problem's continued existence. The only real victims were the peddlers unfortunate enough to be marked by the brigands.

However, at one point, this bandit problem — already reeking of bloody money — took a turn for the worse.

One of the bandit gangs started kidnapping children from Gideon and the nearby villages.

They demanded ransom money for every child, and those with unpaid ransoms were simply never returned. Some relatives didn't get their children back even after paying, while others only received shredded pieces of their corpses. It all seemed like a sick joke.

Naturally, the parents of the children requested to have the Adventurers' Guild eliminate those bandits, and, of course, the guild accepted it.

The officials of the Adventurers' Guild believed that the kidnappers had someone particularly powerful among them. Thus, they gathered and dispatched a party made up of several excellent tian adventurers. It was a group that could even fell a Pure Dragon.

Everyone believed that — regardless of whether the kidnappers had capable people among them — the party would eliminate the bandit gang and bring back any children that were still alive. The party members themselves were certain of that, as well.

The party's leader — famous for his dashing looks — set out on the quest while waving goodbye to the people seeing him off. The intrepid smile on his face made everyone — the guild's officials, other adventurers, and, of course, the inhabitants of Gideon — all the more certain that they would return successful.

The following day, the leader's half-eaten face was placed outside the steps of the guild hall. It was accompanied by a paper saying "Seconds, please," along with a number of small fingers, one finger for every kidnapped child.

Though perplexed by this unexpected turn of events, the Adventurers' Guild quickly made their next move. Their plan was to gather several adventurer parties and annihilate the bandit gang through human-wave tactics. Among the adventurers — numbering nearly a hundred — there were even some Masters. The guild's Masters were absolutely certain that they would emerge victorious.

Three days later, a resurrected Master came back to report what happened. "They killed us all. It just can't be done," he said.

According to him, most of the enemies were absolute weaklings, but two of them were ridiculously strong.

One was a horse-man undead, while the other was a large, ox-headed man. Their power was far beyond that of normal tians, and it was fair to say that they were what had killed most of the adventurers.

With that report, the guild's master realized that this wasn't a job for adventurers. He contacted the knights responsible for the area around Gideon, but the army couldn't act due to the area being close to the border with Caldina.

Even Gideon's local champion — Super Gladiator Figaro — rejected the request, despite being able to take care of the matter all by himself.

The Adventurers' Guild had exhausted all their options, leaving them unable to do anything. Every now and then, some stronger sorts would accept the request and head out to eliminate the bandits, but they would always end up as corpses and were sent back to the guild along with fingers of the children.

This tragedy continued for a year, and the Adventurers' Guild eventually stopped making the request appear in their catalogs.

Thus, the bandits in question — the Gouz-Maise Gang — were still active in the Cruella Mountain Belt.

◆

It was happening in the gloomy cellar of an abandoned fortress.

"Third this month. Payment received. No relevant materials. To be returned." The man mumbled something while looking at an old desk in a piercingly-cold room thick with suffocating moisture.

"Fourth this month. Payment not received. Relevant materials found. Turned to materials."

He looked through the documents, spoke those words, and wrote something down on the ledger in his hand. It was much like a ledger one would use in a business, and the one under his hand wasn't the only one on the table.

Gloomy as the idea might've been, it seemed as though he had only placed them there just for the sake of having them around, and the man wouldn't deny that idea.

"Fifth this month. Payment received. Relevant materials found. Head to be returned after turning to materials." With those words, the man stood up and walked to a neighboring room.

The way he walked was curious. His upper half was that of a human, but the bottom half was that of a horse. The man was a humanoid creature known only as "horse-man."

Just as there were human-horse mix *monsters* known as centaurs, so there were human-horse mix *humans* known as horse-men. An average monster would have its name pop up above its head, but that didn't apply to the man.

Therefore, this horse-man was, in fact, humanoid...

...regardless of just how inhuman his appearance and mental workings were.

"This is the one," he said.

The room had cages in it, and inside there were a number of small animals. They were the man's commodities. The small animals were all asleep and thus completely oblivious to the man's presence.

The horse-man removed the small animal from the fifth cage and placed it on the stony floor of his own room. On the floor, there was a magic circle the man had drawn. The man fixed the shackles, which were chained to the floor, on the small animal's limbs. He took out a black crystal.

"_____"

As he whispered something, the magic circle began to shine, and it released small amounts of purple lightning.

At the very same moment, the small animal woke up.

"GYAAAAHHHHH!"

The shriek that escaped its mouth was thick with anguish.

It tried to raise its body up, but the manacles binding it were not so accommodating. As the metal on its limbs tore through its skin, the small animal's body spasmed and hit its back to the stony floor in a futile attempt to break out.

This continued for a long five minutes...

"Mo...mmy..."

...and at the end, the small animal — the miserable little human child — breathed its last.

"This is less than I expected," the horse-man said, looking at the crystal in his hand.

Then he cut off the corpse's head with a large blade he had prepared, stuffed it into a bag, and threw it into a basket that said "To be returned." The rest of the body was carefully put into a container saying "Materials."

Then — as if what had just happened was nothing special — the man returned to the table and continued filling in the ledger.

No one who knew the ledger's contents would ever compare it to those used in business. At this point, it was nothing but a cursed book containing the fates of countless children.

"Sixth this month. Payment not received. No relevant materials. Dispose. Gouz!"

In response to the man's call, something within the darkness began to move. "Ahh…"

The creature referred to as "Gouz" — a large man with an ox's head and demonic fangs — reached into one of the cages and grabbed a little girl by her arm. She was sleeping and continued to do so even as he dragged her across the floor.

Many would say that she would've been better off if she continued sleeping. However, Gouz didn't allow that. Gently — like a parent or a close friend — he tapped on her cheek.

The little girl stirred and woke up…

"They taste better when they're scared, y'know," he grinned.

…and her flesh was rendered from bone. Eaten alive.

By the time Gouz was done with his snack, the horse-man was done filling in the ledger.

"Gouz, don't make such a mess," he said.

"Gahahah!" the ox-head laughed. "Maise, this place is basically painted with the brats' blood and other fluids! I couldn't make it worse if I wanted to!"

"I'm talking about your saliva. It reeks."

"That so? Well, I'll try to be careful, then."

The horse-man — Maise — sighed at Gouz's half-hearted and unreliable response and changed the subject.

"That's today's set done," he said. "Gouz, after we go through tomorrow's set, we're leaving this place."

"Huh? We are?" asked the ox-head.

"Yes," answered the horse-man. "That event is starting in Gideon in just two days. Some of those who will gather for it might try to eliminate us. It would be far too troublesome."

"Masters, huh?" sighed Gouz. "Why not just kick their non-serious asses?"

"Because we can't," curtly replied Maise. "We could handle those with high-rank jobs, but Superiors and their Superior jobs would be far too challenging. Also…"

He momentarily stopped talking, merely to emphasize the words that followed.

"…they stand where we are aiming for."

Maise's words — which had some sort of certainty to them — made Gouz laugh out loud. "Gehahahaha! You're not wrong there."

"Ah, it just hit me," added the ox-head. "You said we're leaving, but what about our underlings? There are, like, a hundred of 'em, and they're still working hard getting the brats and whatnot."

Gouz's question made Maise's eyes — empty sockets where a wisp-like fire popped up and disappeared — light.

"We're taking them with us, of course," said the horse-man.

"Gahahah! Hope they all fit!"

Gouz was a man-eating ox-head demon with a high-rank job from the gladiator grouping: Strong Gladiator.

Maise: a grudge-wielding undead horse-man with a high-rank job from the necromancer grouping — Lich.

They were the Gouz-Maise Gang.

They were Gideon's most feared band of kidnappers and murderers.

Chapter One ⟩ A Morning in Gideon

Paladin Ray Starling

Most large cities in the Kingdom of Altar — the royal capital included — were encircled by a large wall. Not only was it a necessary structure that protected against monsters and attacks from other countries, it also separated the worlds inside and out.

Duel City Gideon, where we had just arrived, was no different.

"Whoa…" I couldn't help but voice my amazement. Beyond the walls — which were similar to the ones in the capital — waited a radically different scenery.

It made me remember how I'd felt when I had first entered Altea. The atmosphere of a hyper-realistic fantasy town was moving, to say the least, and Gideon was making me experience it all over again.

The air here was thick with people's enthusiasm. I had a feeling that most of it came from the very middle of the metropolis — the Great Central Arena of the duel city, towering right before my eyes. Ancient Rome's Colosseum was 200 meters in diameter and 50 meters in height, yet Gideon's pride and joy seemed to be more than twice the size of that.

According to a sign hanging near the gates to Gideon, there were twelve smaller arenas evenly spaced out around the city, and every single one of them was active daily. The sign also said that the Great Central Arena was often used for various events.

With all the liveliness here in Gideon, I found it hard to believe that this city was part of a kingdom that had recently experienced a crippling blow in a war and was forced to the verge of defeat.

I looked around and saw a number of humanoid races I didn't encounter much back in the capital. Some had beast-like ears, others had dragon-like horns... There were even some fairies, so petite they only went up to my knees. They seemed to be this world's Demi-Humans — a staple for every fantasy work.

As I watched them, I noticed that there were both tourists and those who actually lived and worked here. Figaro hadn't been lying when he'd said this place was lively.

"What an energetic city," said Rook.

"It's only natural, since this area isn't close to the kingdom's border with Dryfe, which is in the north," Marie said. She began explaining why. "The countries close to Gideon are Caldina and Legendaria. The latter signed a treaty of commerce with Altar, while the former is a full ally, so this city gets many tourists from both."

She showed us a map to illustrate what she'd explained. In the center of the map was Gideon; to the east, a mountain belt, followed by Caldina; and to the south, there was Legendaria. To the west, there was a small patch of land followed by the open sea, while to the north, there was the capital.

"Not only is Gideon positioned in a safe spot — you can also count all the gladiators fighting in the arenas as its soldiers," Marie continued. "It wouldn't be an exaggeration to say that Gideon is the strongest city in the kingdom."

I see, I thought. *That makes it the safest city in the Kingdom of Altar.*

I could only assume that many people who'd escaped from the capital had chosen this as their destination. After all, in the catalog of the capital's guild, there had been many escort requests from people searching for a safe refuge.

However, there were still merchants like Alejandro, who would go out of their way to stock up in the capital. We and that merchant had gone our separate ways at the entrance to Gideon, but since he'd wished to thank us properly, he'd invited us to visit his shop whenever we had the time.

"Now, let's go to the Adventurers' Guild," said Marie. "We have to finish the quest and report that Gardranda was eliminated."

Rook and I were quick to agree, and we all made our way to Gideon's Adventurers' Guild.

The ceiling inside it was higher than it was in the capital's guild. The entrance was larger, too. The designers were probably being considerate of the larger races inhabiting and visiting this city.

Anyway, we completed the delivery quest without any problems. The reward was 30,000 lir. We split it evenly and got 10,000 lir each. It was a nice amount, no doubt about it. However, we ran into some problems when claiming the reward we were supposed to get for taking care of Gardranda.

Proving that we'd done it wasn't difficult at all. We simply had to go to a special counter and show them the MVP special reward: The Miasmaflame Bracers, Gardranda.

Items of this type were always named after the defeated UBM, had qualities that fit the MVP, and couldn't be transferred in any way. Thus, the fact that I possessed the item with Gardranda's name on it could only mean that I had been the most valuable player in Great Miasmic Hobgoblin, Gardranda's elimination.

Of course, it was also possible to prove such things by going through a thorough inquiry. It was only natural, considering that not every bounty was a UBM.

And so, though we got the reward money without any trouble, we found the amount to be quite problematic.

It amounted to a total of 1,000,000 lir. That was the equivalent of 10,000,000 yen, which was quite a fortune. It got us to sit around a table in the guild and intensely argue about how we would split it.

"Oh, come on, now!" I raised my voice. "Let's just all take a third and be done with it!"

"No!" said Marie. "I already took the money for the potions I used, so there's no reason for me to have any more! I didn't participate in the battle at all! You two should just split it in half!"

"I didn't fight Gardranda, either!" cried Rook. "I could never accept the same amount as Ray! He should just take it all, honestly!"

The three of us were fiercely arguing in favor of reducing the amounts we would get.

First, Marie had been given approximately 100,000 lir of the reward to make up for the Elixir she'd thrown at me and other medicines she'd used on the people in the carriages. She'd been apprehensive about accepting it, saying that she'd chosen to use those items on her own volition, but I'd insisted, and she'd soon caved. With that settled, we'd had 900,000 lir left, and that was when things had gotten fiery.

I had argued that it had been the result of us acting as a party, and insisted that we all take a third each.

Marie had insisted that she didn't deserve or need more than what she'd gotten for the medicine.

Rook had stated that he didn't deserve any money because he hadn't participated in the battle against Gardranda.

I sincerely believed that they both were invaluable in the victory against the demon, so I really wanted them to take what was rightfully theirs.

"Honestly, I already got the MVP special reward, so maybe I shouldn't take any of it," I said.

"That would take you beyond simple selflessness and quickly make you look like an unreasonable lunatic," commented Nemesis.

I was being completely serious, yet Nemesis looked at me like I was an idiot. Rook and Marie, too, seemed thoroughly perplexed by my suggestion.

"Hey, these things are downright insane," I said. "I really can't let myself take much after getting something *this* good."

I raised my hands to show off the things on them. These two-tone colored bracers — one red, other dark purple — were inside my inventory after we had defeated Gardranda.

The description in the equipment window went like this:

Miasmaflame Bracers, Gardranda
Legendary item
A legendary item embodying the concepts surrounding the three-faced demon of flame and miasma.
In addition to being extremely tough, it increases the physical strength of the wearer.
This item cannot be transferred or traded.
No level limit.

It actually gave a 100% bonus to STR, and had more defense than all my other armor combined. Not only that, but it also allowed me to use the skills "Purgatorial Flames" and "Hellish Miasma," which were probably much like the attacks used by the UBM itself. There was also a skill that I couldn't read for some reason, one that simply said "???".

They were insanely good, no doubt about it.

Not only did they seem to be worth more than 300,000 lir — they'd probably go for more than the whole reward for defeating Gardranda.

I mean, it's a "legendary" item, I thought.

"I know I'm the MVP and all, but taking the reward after getting *these* would be far too much," I said.

We would have lost the battle against Gardranda if Marie hadn't provided support with her items. Rook, too, had done a great job holding back Audrey — who had originally been the demon's mount.

We wouldn't have achieved victory if it hadn't been for them, so I thought I was fair in insisting that my contributions were worth only a third of the reward.

"...I understand," said Marie. "But I think I have a better idea." She lightly hit the table. "First of all, Ray, you're getting 300,000, and that's final. If *you* don't accept that money, no one here has the right to have any of it. Now, Rook, I know you don't want to take as much as Ray, so let's cut it by half and give you at least 150,000. And before anyone tells me off for not taking anything, I'll be satisfied with just 50,000, thank you very much."

Rook and I weren't against that split, so that was 500,000 lir taken care of. However, there was still 400,000 lir left.

"We shall use the rest as a party," said Marie.

"By that, you mean...?" I raised an eyebrow.

"You could call it a little lesson for future reference," she answered.

What is she talking about? I thought.

"For now, just leave it all to me," she continued. "I would like you to gather here in the afternoon after three days game time. Is that okay with both of you?"

Three days game time was just one day in reality.

"No problems here," said Rook.

"I don't have any plans for tomorrow, either, but what are you planning?" I asked.

"Let's have it be a little secret for the sake of surprise," said Marie. "Oh, but if you don't like this idea of mine, just say so. I'll give your money back at once."

"No, it's fine by me," I said. I had absolutely no intention of taking any more, so I just let Marie do her thing.

"Then with that, we're done splitting the money," she said. "Good job on finishing this quest, you two."

"Yeah, thanks for the help," I said.

"Thank you very much," said Rook.

And so ended the first quest we had taken up as a party.

We had a small celebration, and by the end, I was so tired that I immediately logged out.

The next day, I logged in soon after waking up.

I'd slept long enough for a whole day to have passed in the game. *Infinite Dendrogram's* tripled time feature was useful and all, but situations like these made it seem a bit confusing and even bothersome. The time here was six o'clock in the morning, and the sun was just beginning to rise.

As soon as I logged in, Nemesis jumped out of the crest on my left hand and greeted me. "Good morning, Master. You sure are early today."

"...Funny, considering that I basically overslept in terms of real life time," I said.

"So what are you doing today?" asked Nemesis. "It's too early for shops to be open."

"Well, I was thinking of doing it after getting some new gear, but I guess I'll have to do the testing first," I answered.

"Testing? Of what?" she asked again.

I raised both my hands before her. "These." They were covered by two pieces of armor. My Miasmaflame Bracers.

Just like the royal capital, most of the kingdom's cities always had their gates open. There were many reasons for that, but one of them was the fact that there were many Masters who were active at night. It would be extremely inconvenient if they were only allowed to pass during the day, and there would be many people who would go out of their way to try to climb over the walls. Thus, the gates were open 24 hours a day. There were three guard shifts, and it reminded me of part-time jobs in convenience stores.

When I passed the northern gate and greeted the guards standing there, they greeted me back in a slightly sleepy manner.

Soon after leaving the city, I was standing in Nex Plains, the same place I had passed through yesterday.

I roamed about looking for a monster I could do the test on, and it didn't take long for me to find a lone Goblin Warrior. I was familiar with this monster, so I could defeat it even if the test failed. A good target, no matter how I looked at it.

"You said you were going to test the bracers, but is there anything specific you had in mind?" asked Nemesis in her sword form.

"Well, these Miasmaflame bracers have skills on them, right? I want to see if they're of any use," I said. "I don't like the idea of having to try them out on something stronger than myself."

I had gotten Vengeance is Mine during the fight with the Demi-Drag and Like a Flag Flying the Reversal while fighting Gardranda, but I couldn't continue to rely on skills I wasn't familiar with to always match my situation and lead me to victory. Testing was important.

Therefore, I decided to test the two skills on the item — Purgatorial Flames and Hellish Miasma. I couldn't use the skill named "???", so that was on hold for now.

One was a flamethrowing skill, while the other was a release of poisonous gas. If I could master them, I would finally have attacks other than standard blows and Vengeance is Mine. Having to use Gems just to cast spells was quite a waste, after all.

"...Oh, it just hit me that I still have some of those Gems," I muttered.

Suddenly, the Goblin noticed I was here and charged at me while swinging his weapon.

"All right, then... Purgatorial Flames." I stretched my hand out to the Goblin and opened my palm flat facing towards it.

A moment later, a demon's mouth opened up on the back of my hand...

"Eh?"

…and it released a fierce stream of crimson fire, painting my vision red.

"AAAGHHHHH!"

Damn, that made my HP go down so fast! I thought. *It's my own attack, so it's not affected by Paladin's Aegis and other defensive skills! Oh, crap! I even got the "Burns" debuff!*

"You fool! Are you trying to kill yourself?! Oh! The Goblin is coming!" shouted Nemesis.

"OAAGHH!"

The damage I'd caused myself had turned this into an extremely dangerous battle. I desperately defended myself against the Goblin's attacks, used a number of skills and healing items, and barely emerged victorious.

Lesson learned. As important as testing was, one always had to consider safety.

◇

"…All right, time to pull myself together and test the Hellish Miasma," I said.

"Are you sure it will work right this time?" asked Nemesis.

"It will," I answered. "…I think."

After a short while of looking for a new prey, I had stumbled upon a bipedal, plant-like monster. The words above it said "Walking Grapevine," and just as they implied, it was literally a walking vine with grapes hanging from it.

"Is that thing even breathing?" asked Nemesis. "Wouldn't it be better to burn it?"

"I'm testing the Hellish Miasma right now. And yes, plants *do* breathe, so it should work," I answered. "Hellish Miasma! Release!"

This time, I made sure to make the back of my hand face the enemy and thus prevent the smoke from hitting myself.

Just as I'd intended, the miasma surrounded the Walking Grapevine... and then a strong gust of wind made it go back to me.

"GYAAAAHHH!"

"I knew this would happen!" shouted Nemesis.

Trying to not breathe any of it in, I escaped the noxious cloud.

Man, that was close, I thought. *I almost got destroyed by my own skill.*

"Now, let's see what the monster thinks of it," I said. I looked as the wind made the miasma disperse to reveal the Walking Grapevine, clearly suffering due to the debuffs.

"It seems to be effective," said Nemesis. "However, it's hard to make it work on windy days, and trying to use it indoors isn't even an option."

"Yeah, I can't deny that it's a difficult skill to use," I said.

As we were having that exchange, something flew right into my mouth.

"Hghuh?!" I accidentally bit and gulped it down. The aftertaste — both sweet and sour — was that of a grape.

A grape, of all things.

Yes, that Walking Grapevine was actually attacking me with its grapes.

"Whot kind ohf attahck ish that?!" I exclaimed in confusion.

"Master, don't talk with your mouth full," said Nemesis.

Seriously, though, what am I supposed to think about this attack? I thought. *The grapes are pretty good, and even if they hit me on the body, they only get me a bit dirty and don't hurt at all—*

"Guh…" My face suddenly contorted.

"Master, what's wrong?! Was that attack poisoned?!" asked Nemesis in perplexion.

Poison? I thought. *Yeah, it was poisoned.*

My stats clearly showed the debuffs that were affecting me. Their names were Poison, Intoxication, and Weakness.

"They're the same debuffs I just gave it…!" I said. Apparently, its fruit had become poisoned by the miasma and I'd gotten its effects transferred to me by ingesting them. I'd had no idea that debuffs could travel like that.

"M-Master!" exclaimed Nemesis. "There's a number of monsters coming this way!"

I looked around and saw some Goblins and beast-type monsters here and there. They were all here because of me — or, rather, the fruit juice on my body.

"I see, so that's the aim of that attack…" I muttered.

And so, still under the effects of the debuffs, I was attacked by a group of monsters which numbered to more than ten.

"We ran into some unexpected trouble, but I think I know how these skills work now," I said.

Despite the tremendous failure on its first use, I had soon found out that Purgatorial Flames was an exceptionally effective skill.

First of all, it was very powerful. It actually did more damage than my standard attacks. I could also continue to channel it as long as I had MP, not to mention that it could apply the Burns debuff or its upgrade — Charring. Just as the name said, it was a debuff that could reduce a burned Goblin's arm to charcoal.

Strong as it might be, however, Purgatorial Flames affected friend and foe alike.

Heck, it includes myself, as well, so I'll have to be really careful when using it, I thought.

Also, its power was lower than that of Gardranda's flames. If it had been the same, the first failure would've blown my head away. I could only assume that Purgatorial Flames was weaker than the original either because it had been reduced to equipment, or because I was simply a weaker creature. Due to the fact that there was a skill I'd yet to unlock, it was quite obvious that I wouldn't be able to master the Miasmaflame Bracers just yet.

And though it had gotten me into the unexpected predicament of getting surrounded by more than ten monsters, the Hellish Miasma test had been successful, as well.

Man, that was tough, I thought. *If I hadn't activated the Reversal, I would be dead by now.*

The only reason I'd survived was because I'd fought the monsters while powered up by the reversed debuffs.

By the time it was over, the Walking Grapevine had succumbed to the Poison and died. I was lucky to have found out that debuffing a monster and then getting those debuffs by ingesting its body parts was counted as a negative effect from the monster.

Though I have no idea if I'll ever find a use for it, I thought. *I don't eat monsters while fighting, after all.*

Whatever the case, I had to be extra careful when using Hellish Miasma.

Oh, I almost forgot to mention. Since the Walking Grapevine had died, the Reversal was no longer effective. Thus, I was currently being tortured by the debuffs.

"Uoghh..." I moaned. "First Heal."

While lying on the ground due to Intoxication and Weakness, I used healing magic to restore my HP, which was being drained by Poison.

Since the Purgatorial Flames were weaker, I had hoped that would apply to Hellish Miasma, as well, but that clearly wasn't the case. It was just about as bad as it had been when Gardranda'd given me these debuffs.

"Perhaps it becomes less effective on stronger creatures," pondered Nemesis. "Your level is low, so it seems like its effect on you is still powerful."

"Y-You might be right..." I muttered.

When examining the way the debuffs were applied and the relationship between Burns and Charring, I began to believe that some debuffs could change depending on how great the cause was. Say someone got attacked by something that applied debuffs, causing the attacked person's debuff "level" to rise and make a debuff appear. Would it really be strange for a continued barrage of such attacks to stack the debuff level and make the illness more serious?

In other words, breathing the miasma for too long might cause some new debuffs to appear, I theorized. *...Not that I'm willing to try it.*

"But man, this is bad," I said. "I might have to go back to the city by crawling on all fours."

"That would be quite unsightly," said Nemesis. "Oh…?"

As I looked to where Gideon was — still lying on the ground — a shadow came over me.

I realized that someone was standing behind me, so I slowly got up and looked at who it was. I wasn't in a hurry because I was still under the effects of the debuffs and could simply feel that the presence wasn't hostile, unlike the Goblins and such.

"…Eh?" I said, startled.

That assumption of mine had turned out to be both correct and wrong. The thing was definitely not a monster. However, it was clearly a creature one had to be cautious with.

"…"

It was a penguin. A large, bear-sized penguin suit was looking down at me.

"Huh?!" I hastily tried to back away, but the debuffs rendered me unable to move as I pleased. Even as I began to panic, the penguin did nothing but continue to watch me, completely immobile.

"…Did Brother Bear get himself a new suit?" asked Nemesis.

"No, it's not my brother," I answered.

However, it didn't seem like a monster or a player killer, either.

It seemed like all it did was observe me.

"What the hell *are* you?" I asked.

"What am I, you ask? Heh heh heh heh… Oops!" In response to my question, the penguin completely destroyed his — the voice was male — silence and immobility and jumped upwards.

After making a number of mid-air spins, he landed and took a V-like pose.

"My name is Fla…MINGO! Call me Dr. Flamingo, if you will."

…*What a weirdo.* I thought.

"Would you say that suits are a signal for oddballs?" asked Nemesis.

We only have two so far, I thought. *If we find a third suited weirdo, I'll accept this theory of yours.*

Putting that aside, however…

"Flamingo?" I raised an eyebrow. "That's a penguin suit, isn't it?"

It reminded me of Adelie Penguins, common to many aquariums. Its primary colors were black and white, and no one with eyes could mistake it for the flashy, pink bird he'd named himself after.

"Who cares about the details?! What matters here is that you seem to be in a pickle! Do drink this!" The penguin reached for his pocket — which was in the suit's stomach area — and took out a medicine bottle with liquid inside it.

"And this is?" I asked.

"A drug that removes debuffs!" he answered. "It instantly takes care of all disease-based status effects!"

I didn't know how to respond. If he wasn't lying, I would gladly chug it down, but I had basically no reason to believe such a blatantly suspicious penguin.

"Isn't this a trap?" asked Nemesis.

I had gone through Lei-Lei's lesson with the fake alcohol and knew the dangers of such offers, but if this penguin had had any intention to hurt me, he would've done it while I was writhing around due to the debuffs. He'd had no reason to prepare a trap for me.

"Thanks." I took the drug from the penguin's hand, activated Reversal just to be on the safe side, and slowly drank it down.

...Hey, this is pretty good, I thought. It had the taste of mixed fruit juice.

Soon after I drank it, the debuffs burdening my body quickly faded away...

"Drank it all, didn't you?" spoke the penguin.

...and, at the same time, I was attacked by a sudden, powerful headache.

"Huh?! You little...!" I growled.

"So it *was* a trap!" exclaimed Nemesis.

The headache made me fall to my knees and grab hold of my head.

"I've been watching you and thinking..." said the penguin. "...'What kind of drug would suit him best?'" The pain continued to get worse.

"It didn't take long for me to come to a conclusion! It simply had to be *this* prototype!" he declared.

Soon enough, the headache became completely unbearable... and then it disappeared as if it had never been there.

"Huh?"

What was that all about? I thought. The headache had faded away and not caused anything to happen.

The penguin that drugged me seemed to be strangely satisfied. Not that I saw his face, but still.

"Hey, what the hell did you make me dri—?!"

"M-Master!" Nemesis cut me off. "Ears! Your ears!"

In response to her words, I reached for my ears, but didn't find anything wrong with them.

"Not *those* ears! The ones above!" she exclaimed.

The ears above? I thought. *But I only have one set of ear—*

Suddenly, I felt something fluffy.

"Hm…?"

What was that strange sensation? I once again reached for the place I'd just touched — the area between the temporal region and calvaria. And again, I felt something fluffy. It was actually kinda pleasant to the touch. It reminded me of the ears of a Siberian husky I used to have…

"YES! I knew those ears would look great on you!" From seemingly nowhere, the penguin took out a full-length mirror. In it, I saw myself…

…with dog ears — as golden as my hair — sticking out of my head.

"…" …*Wha*— "WHAT THE HELL IS THIS?!"

"I happen to be a humble Researcher, and I merely wanted to test my very own Animal Ear Drug," the penguin explained. "When I went around to look for a convenient guinea pig, I stumbled upon you, just lying there on the ground. Not letting this divine opportunity go to waste, I mixed and blended a drug that removed your status effects with the drug I wished to test. My evaluation didn't fail me! The Animal Ear Drug was a success, and the dog ears look absolutely perfect on you! …I'm sorry, I am *so* sorry! I'll genuflect and apologize, so could you please withdraw your sword? You'll tear my suit! Please stop! It might reach my throat!"

I pushed Nemesis against the mad scientist penguin's throat as I found out that I'd been used as his guinea pig.

Forgive me, Lei-Lei, I thought. *I deserve this for failing to follow your advice. But man, isn't this a bit too much?*

"I'm not too big on fashion, but there are three things I've decided to never wear under any circumstances," I spoke.

"A-And those are?" asked Nemesis.

"Glasses, girl's clothing, and animal ear headbands."

Naturally, this turn of events was quite upsetting.

"Master," said Nemesis, "you are more averse to glasses than girl's clothing?"

"Glasses are great," said the penguin. "This pair, for example, gives you various skills and—"

"Shut up!" I cut his words short.

"Th-That sounded like you intend to kill him," commented Nemesis.

"I'm shorryy!" cried the penguin.

No glasses, not ever, I thought.

"Well... what the hell do I do now?" I tried to hide the dog ears with some random headgear, but I couldn't equip anything. They all got rejected like magnets of the same pole. I brought up my equipment window, and it said that I already had "Dog Ears" equipped on my head. Apparently, as is normal in most such games, you could only wear a single piece of equipment in each slot.

By the way, these Dog Ears had no bonuses or skills on them. It was an item that only changed my appearance. However, just like a generic cursed object straight out of your average RPG, it couldn't be removed through the equipment window.

There were also no relevant status effects to accompany that function, and Reversal couldn't do anything about it, either.

"How do you fix this?" I asked.

"It's growing out of your head, so you can't just take it off," said the penguin. "It's like a sub-type of hair makeovers."

Man, that's annoying, I thought.

"Oh, but it should disappear after some time," he continued. "If I had to guess, it will happen sometime in the evening."

"By which time standard?" I asked.

"This world's, of course."

That was the equivalent of ten hours here or three hours in reality.

"Then I guess I'll just log out until that time comes," I said. I didn't want anyone I knew to see me like this.

"Oh no, time when you're logged out wouldn't count," the penguin said. "It would be boring if it did."

...This mad penguin just said the word "boring," didn't he?

"Hhaah… All right," I sighed, resigned. "Guess I'll just continue like this, then…"

Having to go about with something like this on my head was somewhat embarrassing. *But when compared to having to wear glasses… hey, I guess this ain't all that bad,* I thought.

"Just *what* did glasses ever do to you?" asked Nemesis.

Not gonna comment.

"By the way, Ray, my boy," spoke the penguin again.

"What is it?" I asked.

"I have but one humble request." The penguin looked at me with a serious face — not that I could see it, but it felt that way — and stated what he wanted of me. "I want to take a screenshot, so could you take off your clothes? Just the top would be fine."

Without saying a word back, I slashed at him.

"Fwahahahah! Farewell!"

The penguin evaded my attack and quickly ran in the direction of the city.

Man, is he fast, I thought. *A penguin has no business being this fleet of foot.*

"What do we even make of oddballs like this…?" asked Nemesis.

"No idea. From the fact that he mentioned screenshots, it's obvious that he's a Master, but… Hm?" I stopped talking and realized something.

I realized that the penguin had called me by my name before he left. And I definitely hadn't introduced myself to him…

After that penguin weirdo gave me the dog-ear drug, I made my way back to the city.

Since Gideon was a place where demi-humans weren't uncommon, the guards didn't make any comments about my new appearance.

I could hear one of them whisper, "Huh? Did that guy have those ears when he greeted us in the morning...? Guess I wasn't fully awake," but that was the extent of it.

"All right, what now?" I asked myself.

Prior to the testing, I'd had plans to go say hello to Alejandro, buy some new equipment, and perhaps even go hunting alongside Rook and Marie, provided they were online. As things were now, however, I didn't want to encounter anyone I knew. Being seen with these dog ears on my head would be downright degrading.

"I don't see why it bothers you that much," said Nemesis.

It'd be weirder if it didn't bother me, I thought. *Imagine a scenario where a good friend suddenly appears before you with a pair of dog ears coming out of his head.*

I was fully confident that such a sight would be etched onto my brain forever.

I'm strongly averse to the idea of that happening, so I don't want to see anyone I kno—

"Ah, Ray, Nemesis. Good morning," a feminine voice reached my ears before I could finish my thought.

I had no words for this situation.

Seriously?! You do this to me right when I was thinking that?! I thought.

"Well, if it isn't Marie," said Nemesis.

"Indeed it is," replied the Journalist.

"Now, Ray, why do you have such a unique look on your fa…" Marie stopped talking and fixed her gaze on the things sprouting out of my head.

Crap, she's staring at them, I silently panicked. *She's seriously eyeballing them.*

I had to clear things up before she thought I was some weirdo who got his kicks from wearing dog ears.

"Marie, just so you know, this isn't my thin—"

"Don't say anything, Ray!" she cut me off.

"Excuse me?!" The vigor in her words made me stiffen up and rendered me unable to continue what I wanted to say. With her gaze still fixed on me, Marie reached into her wristband-shaped inventory and took something out. It was…

"A sketchbook and… a pen?" I looked at the items with questioning eyes.

Just like she had during the minion capacity explanation, Marie began drawing something at an incredible speed. I wasn't knowledgeable about the subject of drawing, but I couldn't help but question if it was really possible for such a coherent picture to have come from such fast movements. With nimble strokes, she drew the outline, the hair, the details on the face and — of course — the dog ears.

"Phew," she sighed. Two minutes later, Marie finally took the pen away from the paper and put up a satisfied expression. On the sketchbook in her hands, there was a ridiculously well-drawn picture of a blond youth with dog ears and no upper clothing.

…Huh? Is this me? But I still have my clothes on, I thought.

"Impressive," said Nemesis.

"Well, yeah, it's good, but… It's good, but I, uh…" I stumbled.

It was definitely a high-quality drawing, but I had no idea how to react to a depiction of a shirtless me with dog ears. The art style was a perfect fit for those monthly magazines that were aimed at teenage boys, but which happened to have a lot of female readers, and that made it even harder for me to comment on it.

"Is there a Drawing skill or something?" I asked.

"It's included among the sense skills, yes, but this is all me," Marie answered.

Oh, so she's good at drawing in real life, I thought.

"So, Ray, how did you end up with such a splendid pair of dog ears?" she asked.

"...A penguin drugged me." I told her the details of my encounter with Mister Flamingo.

"I must say, that penguin has some great taste," said Marie. "I'll make sure to buy some of that Animal Ear Drug if it ever gets on the market."

"Not that I'd stop you, but... are you serious?" I asked.

"Very," she answered. "By the way, Ray. Dog ears look great on you, but I think that tiger or fox ears wou—"

"Whoa, now! Don't think of using it on me!" I cut her off.

"...Tch."

Did this shady Journalist just click her tongue?! I thought in disbelief.

"Anyway, you said that the effect wears off in the evening," she said, changing the subject. "What do you plan to do until then?"

"I was thinking of paying a visit to Alejandro's shop, but I can't really do that with these things popping out of my head," I answered. I didn't want people to see them.

Although it may be a lost cause, considering they've already been seen by someone I know, I thought.

"Hmm, I really don't think it's such a big deal," said Marie. "You shouldn't be so self-conscious about them."

"But—"

"You'd be hard-pressed to find a tian who'd be surprised by a Master who suddenly grew a pair of animal ears," she cut me off and explained. "To most tians, we Masters are creatures that exist outside the boundaries of common sense."

Is that how it is? I asked myself. *Well, now that I think about it, the King of Destruction destroyed a whole forest in a single night, so it's perfectly reasonable for tians to see us that way.*

"Guess I'll go to Alejandro's place, then," I sighed.

"I'm still busy with something, so I can't join you," said Marie.

"Busy?" I asked.

"Various preparations and all that," she responded, but didn't make anything clear. "Speaking of which, don't forget to meet up with me tomorrow afternoon."

"Yeah, I remember the plan," I said. "What are you preparing, anyway?"

"It's a secret," she answered. "See you tomorrow!"

With those words as her last, Marie ran off towards an uncertain direction. I couldn't help but wonder what kind of surprise she had in store for us.

After splitting up with Marie, Nemesis and I made our way to the shop address Alejandro had given us yesterday, which was located in Gideon's fourth district.

Gideon was a circular city split into twelve districts — making it seem much like a sliced cake — and the fourth was an area focused on trade. Making my way through the bazaars while trying not to get lost among all the people and other things, I somehow arrived at Alejandro's shop.

The large building had a sign that said "The Alejandro Company." I peeked inside and saw a variety of goods being sold. Obviously, there were weapons, armor, and healing items, but I also noticed works of art such as paintings and statues. There were fruit and other foods, as well, and they created quite a contrast with the rows of Jewels on display. The place was much like a department store.

"Good morning," I said as I came in. A moment later, a young girl — clearly an employee — ran up to me.

"Is Alejandro here right now?" I asked.

"Oh! You're the Master from the day before yesterday!" she exclaimed. "Thank you very much for what you did back then! I'll call the owner immediately!" The girl trotted off deeper into the shop.

From her words, it was pretty obvious that she had been one of the tians riding the carriages when Gardranda had attacked. I couldn't tell if I'd seen her back then, though. Things had been pretty hectic, after all.

"What a fidgety young girl," said Nemesis. "From the air about her, I assume that she has the makings of a 'klutz.'"

Not sure how I feel about summarizing people with a single word, I thought. *What word would you summarize yourself with, Nemesis?*

"Goddess," she answered with no hesitation.

Well, your name is that of a goddess, yeah, but I'd say you're better summed up as an "old loli ha-" I thought willfully.

"Hey! What were you about to think just now?!" Nemesis exclaimed.

"Ha ha ha, don't be so loud," I said. "You'll disturb the other customers."

"That laugh was so forced!" she shouted, seeing right through me.

As we were fooling around, Alejandro walked out from the shop's inner quarters.

"Well, if it isn't Mr. Ray," he said. "You are most welcome here."

"Hello," I greeted him. "Since you insisted that I pay a visit, I came to take a look at your wares."

"Oh, please do," he said. "Look at them for as long as you like. You get a discount on everything I have."

"Thank you," I said.

I had to get a lot of new gear appropriate to my current level, so a discount was very welcome.

Also, there was something I couldn't help but notice. The female employee and Alejandro weren't making any comments about my dog ears. Sure, the girl gave them a few involuntary glances, but she didn't say anything at all. Alejandro, on the other hand, acted as though the ears didn't even exist. A pro if I ever saw one.

Perhaps Marie was right about tians not being mindful of such things happening with Masters.

I was thankful for that. Having to explain the dog ears to every single person I encountered would've been really annoying.

Now, I can only hope they disappear before I meet Rook again, I thought.

"Oh, look, it's Ray and Nemesis," said someone in the shop. "Good morning. Nice to see that you're already logged in."

"Helloo," followed a feminine voice. "Oh? Why do you have those ears, Ray?"

I turned to see Rook and Babi, who had — apparently — been shopping here before we came in.

I had no words. *This is the second time today that my hope has died the very moment I created it,* I thought. *Are these dog ears cursed or something?*

"If you consider everything that's happened ever since you logged in this morning, the cursed item here might be the Miasmaflame Bracers, not the ears," said Nemesis.

...You have a point, I thought.

"Ray, how did you end up with that nice pair of ears?" asked Rook.

"It's a result of this and that happening because of so on and so on," I said.

"Surely you're not expecting him to understand that," commented Nemesis.

"I see," said Rook. "You ended up like that because a shady person tricked you into drinking some drug, right?"

"He actually got it right?!" Nemesis and I couldn't hide our surprise.

Are you an esper or something? I thought.

"No, this isn't a superpower or anything like that," he answered to my thought. "This level of 'mind reading' is easy once you get the hang of it."

"How can you call it easy when you're talking to my thoughts as naturally as Nemesis does?!" I asked, still perplexed.

"Ohh... what a heavy blow to my identity." Shocked for some reason, Nemesis fell to her knees.

"That's pretty amazing, Rook," I said. "You'd be unbeatable when playing old maid."

"Old maid, huh…" he said. "I don't think this ability of mine would be this precise with anyone I don't know, though. The most I can do with strangers is tell how they feel and notice if they have any ulterior motives."

That's still pretty amazing, I thought.

After Rook surprised us with his special ability, we began looking at the wares on sale here.

"Why are you here, anyway?" I asked him. "To say hi and buy some new gear, I assume?"

"Yes," he answered. "Not just for me and Babi, either. I found out that I can get weapons for Marilyn and Audrey, as well. Also, we went hunting yesterday, so I have some drops to sell."

So there's monster gear here, too, huh? I thought. *This shop sure has a wide variety of items.*

"Hunting, eh?" I said. "What level are you now?"

"48," he answered.

…H-He's about to reach the maximum level a low-rank job can get, I thought. *It's almost two times greater than my level. How am I supposed to feel about this?*

"Looks like someone got real busy during the day I was offline…" I muttered.

I could only assume that having Marilyn and Audrey had made his hunting that much more effective. Heck, Rook and Babi were absolute terrors in large-scale battles by themselves.

"I'm about to reach level 50, so I'll have to start working towards switching to a high-rank job soon," said Rook.

"Do you have anything in mind?" I asked.

"Yes, I did my research and found out that a Pimp's high-rank job is called the 'Lost Heart,'" he answered.

Lost Heart, eh? I thought. It was a reference to the Japanese word used to describe a person who'd lost all the eight virtues as they were presented in works such as *The Eight Dog Chronicles.* The term also referred to people who managed brothels. Quite the unique naming choice.

"Here are the requirements." Rook took out a Catalog and showed me the Lost Heart's page.

Requirement no. 1: Reach level 50 as Pimp.
Requirement no. 2: The sum total of all underling female monster and slave stats must be above a certain point.
Requirement no. 3: The total money gained by making the underling female monsters and slaves work must be above 1,000,000 lir.

"I see," I said. Unlike Paladin, it didn't have any requirements that involved human relations or some special victories. In fact, everything could be achieved by simply playing Pimp for a certain amount of time. These requirements could've been one of the reasons why it wasn't classified as a battle-focused job.

Even though Rook makes it look far more formidable than most battle jobs, I thought.

"I'm about to reach level 50, and the second requirement is already fulfilled," said Rook. "The third one is gonna take a while, though."

"Yeah, that seems like a lot of work," I agreed.

Is it even possible for a Pimp to make money by using creatures such as Marilyn and Audrey? I thought.

"I feel like they would be very efficient in construction sites," said Rook.

I said, "I think that one of the retro games my brother owns had some tamed monster running around a construction site… Hm?"

I belatedly noticed that Rook was wearing a different outfit than he had yesterday. It was a coat that seemed to emit a strange, silver shine.

Well, this looks new, I thought.

"That's an awesome-looking coat, Rook," I said. The details on the décor were elaborate, and the metallic gleam was damn cool.

Its sleeves had different lengths, which made it seem very stylish, and Rook — handsome as he was — made it all come together in the best of ways. He hadn't been wearing it yesterday, so I could only assume that he'd gotten it while I was offline.

"Oh, yes. I like Liz a lot," he said.

Enough to give it a name? I raised an eyebrow.

Suddenly, the coat seemed to move in an unnatural manner. I had no idea why, but the movement seemed somehow happy.

While doing this and that, I finished choosing everything I needed. Since I was going to wear the Miasmaflame Bracers no matter what, I didn't go for set armors like the Riot series items.

In my case, one of the most important pieces of equipment was the chest armor, and since Rook looked really cool in that coat of his, I went for a coat-type piece, as well. It had the name "Blaze Metal Scale Coat."

It was created by taking a coat made from the skins of red, wolf-type monsters and strengthening it with many metal scales. It had two skills on it — "Fire Affinity" and "Fire Resistance." The former increased the damage of my fire-based attacks by 10%, while the other reduced the damage I took from fire by the same amount, giving it good synergy with Purgatorial Flames. Sure, it was a luxury item that'd cost me a whole 80,000 lir, but I had no regrets about choosing it.

I got some other equipment to go with it and made my way to the counter to buy it all.

"Eh?" Right next to the counter, there was a device you'd often see in reality.

It was a rectangular case with many round capsules inside it and a lever on its side. By putting money inside it, you could pull on the lever and make one of the capsules pop out.

It was basically a gacha vending machine.

Gacha vending machines had existed since long before I was born.

I could remember when I used to go to the machines dedicated to my favorite anime or games, pop in 100 yen, pull the lever, and get a random toy related to those series. It was fun because you never knew what you were going to get, and because of that, those memories were dear to me.

However, *in-game* gacha machines were a completely different beast.

Some time ago, there used to be a game genre known as "social games." They could be played on mobile devices and PC browsers, and you could start them without paying any money whatsoever.

Social games were many and varied. Some were fantasy games with equipment systems, while others revolved around monster growing, robot squad creation, or even idol producer work. The games were free, but if the players wished to get high-quality weapons, armor, monsters, robots, or idols, they had to pay additional money.

The most popular method of distributing such treasures was the real money gacha machine. For about 300 yen, the player could pull the virtual machine's lever and get a random item. The items had levels of rarity, and the rarest items of all had the lowest chances of popping out.

Rarity was often related to quality, too. To either win at the games, boast to others, or simply to enjoy their idols, the players would pull the lever. They would do it over and over until they got what they wanted.

However, it was all just data. The companies would never lose anything, no matter how many high-quality, high-rarity pulls the players got. Many players' desire to get the good stuff only increased with every bad thing they pulled, making them throw even more money at the game.

As a result, there had been many players who would spend 100,000 yen on the games every month. Some would even go above and beyond and break the 1,000,000 barrier.

It had been a very real, very dark time, indeed...

With that in mind, the gacha before me takes lir instead of real money, so it's not a big deal if I pull it once or twice, right? I thought.

"...I see that all those thoughts just now were nothing but a big excuse to do it," said Nemesis.

"Well, yeah, I *want* to pull it, after all," I said. I really enjoyed the excitement involved in pulling on gachas and buying random card packs.

All right, back to the thing before me... I thought and looked at the machine. Though its shape was familiar, there were several differences between it and the gachas I knew.

First of all, it was possible to choose the amount of money you wanted to put in. There was a short line before it, and I noticed that some threw single 100 lir coins, while others went in with as much as 10,000 lir.

According to the explanation on the machine, the items that could pop out had rarities from S to F.

Rank C items were worth as much as the money put in.

Rank F — the lowest rank — items were worth only 1% of the money put in.

Rank S — the highest rank — items were worth 100+ times more than the money put in.

The minimum amount of money you could put in was 100 lir, while the maximum was 100,000.

As was natural, low risk meant low reward and high risk meant high reward.

"But doesn't that make it hard to keep track of the items inside and manage the quality of what pops out?" I asked an employee, and the answer I got was one I'd never have expected.

"It doesn't work the way you think," she said. "While it is true that we manage this magic item itself, we have nothing to do with the prizes inside or the money used on it."

According to her, this gacha machine had originally been a rare item found in the Tomb Labyrinth.

It wasn't a one-of-a-kind, either. There were records of other people getting these, and some had tried to take them apart and take the prizes by force. Apparently, the effort involved was insane, and yet those who succeeded had found out that the inside of the machine was completely empty.

Thus, everyone had begun to assume that the money offered to it made the machine magically summon an appropriate item. And since it was impossible to retrieve the money used, the gacha definitely wasn't a part of any successful business model.

"However, the owner believes that it works to attract customers, so we keep it here for everyone's convenience," said the employee. "We also made it a rule that only paying customers can use it."

A wise decision, indeed, for it created a decent flow of money from those who only came here for the machine. I now had no doubts that Alejandro was highly skilled as a manager.

"How did he come to have it, anyway?" I asked.

"When its previous owner ran out of money, he had to part with a lot of property," she said. "This was among the items, and our owner bought it."

"…And the reason for the previous owner going broke was…?"

"…Exactly what you imagine," she said.

So he went broke because he pulled on this thing a bit too much, huh? I thought. That might've been another reason why Alejandro was using it for nothing more but attracting customers.

Anyway, I'd grown interested in the gacha machine, so I thanked the employee that told me about it and took my place at the end of the line.

"So, how much do you plan on spending?" asked Nemesis.

"100,000 li—GUH!"

The moment I answered, she hit me with a blow to my stomach. It came from a really good angle, so it actually made me bend forward.

"How can you let yourself use such a great amount of money right after hearing about someone who lost it all because of it?!" she exclaimed.

"I-I know that 100,000 lir is a lot, but I might pull something really good if I'm lucky..." I said.

"This reeks of a scenario where you get something worthless, if you ask me."

Well, if something like that happens, we'll have something to look back at and laugh about later down the line, I thought.

She sighed. "I hope you don't regret this."

"I'm sure I won't," I said.

Soon enough, it was my turn, so I put ten 10,000 lir coins into the gacha. Once done with that, I pulled the lever, making the machine release a single capsule. The thing had the letter C on it. According to the explanation, the thing inside had the same value as the money I'd put in, so it wasn't a loss.

Excitedly, I opened the capsule and made the item inside it pop out.

Tomb Labyrinth Exploration Permit.

Seeing the familiar item made me drop to my knees.

"Ohh... nooooooo..." I groaned. I could almost hear the thing greet me with a smug "Hey there! it's been a while!"

"Oh dear, a double," said Nemesis.

Well yeah, it's worth 100,000 lir, but... but I... I moaned silently.

"Rook... take it," I said, presenting the paper to him.

"Are you sure? Isn't this a decent pull?" he asked.

"It is, but I already have one, and you don't need more than one..."

Hell, being a Paladin, I don't need even one... I thought.

"Th-Thank you," Rook said gratefully. "Umm, shall we go explore it sometime?"

"That's a good idea..." I replied with little enthusiasm. It really *was* a good idea, though, since I hadn't gone beyond the first floor there.

All right, time to pull myself together, and...

"One more," I said.

"Haven't you learned your lesson?!" exclaimed Nemesis.

"Come on! There's no way I'll get another one of the Permits! I'm sure I'll pull something good this time!" I said.

"That's what every gambler thinks before losing it all!"

Despite Nemesis' disapproval, I stood in the line again and got ready for a second try.

Like last time, I went with 100,000 lir. Considering the total cost of the equipment I was buying, this was my last chance.

I pulled on the lever while praying to God, Buddha, or whatever was listening.

And the result was...

"...What?" I raised an eyebrow.

The capsule had popped out as normal, but the rarity displayed on it wasn't even in the range of S to F.

It simply said "X."

Is this above S? Or is the X actually a cross that makes it as worse than F? I was thoroughly confused. There was a little warning on it, saying, "Open only in spacious areas." I asked an employee about it, and she said that warning appeared on any capsules that contained something large, like a carriage. That meant that this capsule had something sizable inside it.

Also, the employee said that this was the first time she'd ever seen a capsule with X rarity on it.

I have no idea how to feel about that, I thought.

Whatever the case, since I could only open it in spacious areas, I chose not to open it inside the shop. I kept it in capsule form and placed it inside my inventory.

Okay, now that I've calmed down, there's something to consider, I thought.

One pull had cost me 100,000 lir.

My new equipment had a combined cost of 110,000 lir.

…That comparison made me aware of just how expensive the pulls were. In terms of rarity, I hadn't really experienced a loss, but I couldn't help but feel off.

"That's what you get for gambling away 200,000 lir," said Nemesis.

I was in no position to say anything to that.

By the time I finished buying my equipment, Rook was trying his own luck on the gacha.

Apparently, seeing me try it got him interested, too.

"…You didn't really have to copy the amount of money I used, though," I muttered. Hoping that his 100,000 wouldn't go to waste, I looked at what he got, and…

And, uh… Huh?

Silence overwhelmed the entire shop. The shock was shared by everyone inside, except Rook.

Nemesis, I, the employees, and the other customers were all at a loss for words.

The capsule in Rook's hand was rainbow-patterned.

It seemed to be made from a mineral so vivid that it looked like a rare item by itself.

Its surface had a large S on it.

Rook had actually pulled something great on his first try.

"Ah, Ray! I think I got something good!" he said.

"C-Congratulations!" My shock made me unintentionally raise my voice.

"Rook, let's hurry up and open it!" Babi cried.

"Y-Yes! Let's find out what you have received!" Nemesis agreed.

Since he'd used 100,000 lir, and the value of an S rarity prize was 100 times greater, the item inside should be worth 100,000,000 lir.

Naturally, something that amazing interested not only us, but the shop employees and other customers, as well.

Rook's capsule didn't have any warnings on it, so he opened it on the spot.

What came out was a pair of gloves, long enough to cover the elbows. Made from a blue, leather-like material, they were decorated by an intricate pattern of golden metal.

""Touch of the Silencer, Veltboule'?" Rook's mutter made me tilt my head.

That naming style was similar to the one on my special reward — "Miasmaflame Bracers, Gardranda." Such special rewards should be impossible to gain without defeating an UBM, and there was no way to transfer them to others, either.

"...Whoa," Rook said. He was looking at the details of the item — Touch of the Silencer, Veltboule — and couldn't hide his amazement.

His face was downright stiff, and it was probably the first time I'd seen him make such an expression.

"So, what kind of item is it, Rook?" I asked.

Looking around, I noticed that some customers — likely Masters and tians with a high Identification skill — seemed as dumbfounded as Rook was.

Okay, now I'm dying to know more about it, I thought.

"Basically, this is an MVP special reward for defeating a UBM," he said.

"Are you serious?" I asked in disbelief.

"Yes," he answered. "Let me tell you the details elsewhere."

After he said that, Rook and I left the shop. As I walked away, I glanced back inside and saw that the line for the gacha had gotten longer and that just about everyone was preparing 100,000 lir.

Apparently, finding out that you could pull UBM special rewards had gotten them all hyped up.

…I hope no one goes broke, I thought.

The place Rook took me to was the room he'd rented at the inn. Rook had clearly learned something that couldn't be heard by other people.

"Basically, this is a special reward that no longer has an owner," he said.

"What do you mean?" I asked.

He explained.

First of all, standard special rewards could only be used by the owner and couldn't be transferred to other people in any way.

However, there was one exception to this rule... and it happened when the owner was a tian who died.

In such cases, the special reward would be automatically retrieved from the body and become either an ultra rare drop in the deeper levels of created dungeons or — as it had been in this case — a high-risk gacha prize.

From that, I could easily understand why he'd gotten all secretive about it.

"You think there'd be more tian-killing if people found out about this, huh?" I asked.

"Yes," he answered.

I had no idea how many special reward-owning tians there were, but I couldn't be certain that there weren't any Masters who would kill them just to increase their chances of getting such items. At the very least, we sure as hell didn't want to be the root cause of such killings. That was the reason why Rook hadn't said that in public.

"Are you sure it didn't slip?" I asked. "What if someone with a high Identification skill saw that part of the description?"

"It wasn't in the item description, but in a personal message," he explained. "No one knows this, I'm sure."

"All's good, then," I said.

Though, now that I think about it, I doubt there would be many Masters willing to take the risk, I thought. Tian-killing could get you on the wanted lists, and there was no guarantee that items gotten this way would ever end up in your hands.

"Here are the details of the item." Rook showed me a window that described the Touch of the Silencer.

[Touch of the Silencer, Veltboule]
[Ancient Legendary Item]
A treasure embodying the concepts surrounding the sphinx famed for being a "mage killer."
In addition to increasing the wearer's magic and special powers, it provides them with a great resistance to mental status effects and attacks.

Just as the description said, the gloves greatly increased the wearer's resistance to mental debuffs and attacks while also giving a large bonus to MP and SP.

"So, what are the effects of the skills on it?" I asked.

"It's pretty interesting," said Rook. "There are two skills on it. I can't read one yet, but the one that I can use now is called 'Silence,' and it cancels any magic-based skills that are in their preparatory stages."

"Oh?" I asked.

Preparatory stages? What does that mean? I thought.

"Apparently, if an opponent is chanting or getting ready to invoke a magic spell, this skill will nullify it," he continued. "But it can't influence any insta-cast skills or magic that has already been cast."

So it's the bane of all casters, huh? Seems like it'll be useful in many scenarios, I thought.

After all, the skill would cancel any spell that hadn't been cast yet. Magic-based jobs would become powerless when going against him mano a mano.

"If it was originally owned by a tian, then... I see how it is," I nodded.

The source of this Touch of the Silencer — the UBM known as Veltboule — had clearly been a creature that specialized in killing casters. It had probably been defeated by a tian who had been strong without having to rely on magic. Later on, the tian had died somehow, and this special reward had ended up in Rook's hands.

"I must say, Rook," Nemesis spoke up, "You are quite a lucky sort."

I couldn't help but agree.

First Marilyn, then Audrey, now this great pull in the gacha… Rook was definitely a very lucky person.

I wonder if that has something to do with him being a good person, I thought.

"But you pulled something good, too, didn't you, Ray?" he said.

"Oh right, I got this thing."

Saying that, I took out the X capsule. I couldn't open it here due to the thing inside being a carriage or something, so I decided to do it after going through the northern gate again.

"I'm going to open it. Care to join me?" I asked Rook.

"I can't. I've been getting messages saying that I need to return to reality," he answered.

"Hm? 'Visitor,' I assume?" I asked.

"'Hunger' and 'Lack of Sleep,' actually," he said. "I've been online since yesterday, hunting monsters and leveling. The only food I've eaten was in-game, and I didn't get any sleep at all."

"Holy crap!" I exclaimed. "Get some food, take a bath, and go to sleep already!"

"Ahaha," he laughed awkwardly. "I'll do just that. I'll make sure to wake up in time for Marie's plan."

"Take care of yourself, man."

After I said that, Rook logged out, so I left his room.

I'd never expected Rook to be enough of a no-lifer to forget his own basic needs.

I guess he's just another student using his spring break for some unreasonable levels of gaming, I thought.

And so, I left the inn. The "spacious area" I was most familiar with was the Nex Plains north of Gideon, so I made my way to the city's northern gate.

"Master," Nemesis said, "shouldn't we have lunch now?"

"Oh yeah, I guess we should," I said. "I'll open the capsule after we do that, then."

I'd probably go hunting in the Nex Plains right after seeing what was inside, so having a meal before that was a good idea.

Since it was noon, most of the nearby restaurants were full, so I chose one that seemed somewhat empty by comparison.

"...Huh?" I said in surprise.

Inside the one I'd chosen, I saw that the shopkeeper was being questioned by a certain group. Wearing full plate mail armor and cloaks that had the Kingdom of Altar's crests on them, they asked something of the shopkeeper while showing him a photo-like object.

Realizing that this was why the shop was so empty, I decided to observe them.

From his ragged voice, I could tell that the one asking questions was in a minor state of panic and that the subject matter was serious. However, looking stumped, the shopkeeper only shook his head in response, making it obvious that he couldn't help them in any way.

After that, a woman from the group tried to calm down her panicked comrade. She was a familiar face.

"Liliana?" I asked.

"Oh? Well, if it isn't Ray," she replied.

It was the Kingdom of Altar's Knights of the Royal Guard, Vice Commander, Paladin Liliana Grandria. I hadn't seen her since I'd left the royal capital, and by some twist of fate, we had happened to meet again here in the city of duels.

As I was busy being surprised by the encounter, Nemesis telepathically told me something ominous.

"I feel some trouble brewing."

Chapter Two ⟩ Back-Alley Cliché

Paladin Ray Starling

Liliana was the first tian I'd ever spoken to. Her responses had been so natural and she'd seemed so alive that I hadn't been able to see her as a tian — as nothing more but an NPC. That feeling was still alive, and even though I knew I was in a game, I couldn't see her as just a game character.

"It has been a while," she said. "I didn't expect to see you here in Gideon."

"Well, I've only been here for about two days," I said.

Probably due to her being my first personal — and physical — contact in this world, my manner of speaking automatically became somewhat courteous. She'd said that it'd been a while since we'd last met, but it had actually only been about eight days.

Now that I think about it, since I've started playing, only ten days have passed in this world and only three in reality, I thought. *Man, this world's days sure are dense.*

"I must ask — why the dog ears?" she asked, looking above my head.

"Please don't," I replied. "Way too much has happened. So, why are you here with such a group?"

Liliana seemed to be somewhat troubled, so I decided to ask her about what was going on. She was surrounded by knights wearing similar armor, flags and unit symbols. Liliana was a Paladin and the

Vice Commander of the Knights of the Royal Guard. From that, I could assume that the people with her were part of the Royal Guard, too.

"Well, Ray, we—"

"Lady Grandria!" one of them cut her words short. "We cannot let any outsiders know of this!"

It was the same man who'd been questioning the shopkeeper. He was glaring at me — or, rather, at the back of my left hand.

"But Sir Lindos, he is one of us — a Paladin," said Liliana.

"He isn't the same as us just because we share a profession," retorted the man. "This is something we have to do without relying on Masters."

It was clear by now that he was Liliana's comrade — a Paladin from the Royal Guard. He also seemed to have a dislike for us players — the Masters.

"It's only fair for him to hate your kind," commented Nemesis.

Indeed. The Kingdom of Altar's Knights of the Royal Guard had reasons to hate us Masters. Altar's Masters were the ones who hadn't helped much during the war, and the Imperium's Masters were the ones who had done the most damage.

The king had even been killed by a Master, so it was only natural for him to hate us.

"But there are things that only they can know," said Liliana. "We are not in a situation that allows us to choose who we get help from."

"...That is reasonable," he said, giving in. "In that case, please search the way you think is best. We will continue looking for her as we were. However, you should only request assistance from those you trust."

"I understand," she nodded. "Be careful in your search."

"Certainly," he said. "Come, men, we're continuing this in the fourth district."

The man Liliana had called Sir Lindos gave the other knights an order, and they all left the shop.

The only ones left inside were Nemesis, Liliana, me, and the shopkeeper, who seemed visibly relieved.

"I see," said Nemesis. "From how he expressed his dislike for Masters, I thought he was an impulsive sort, but it seems that he's malleable when he needs to be."

Or maybe the situation is just grave enough for a Master-hating knight to accept a Master's help, I thought.

"I am sorry, Ray. Sir Lindos isn't a bad person or anything, but…" said Liliana.

"No need for that," I said. "He seemed to be in a hurry."

"Yes, about that… there is something I'd like to ask you." With those words, Liliana took out a single photo.

It gave me a minor déjà vu, making me remember the first time I'd met her. However, the person on the photo was different this time.

"Have you seen this girl anywhere?" she asked.

The person on the photo was a young girl. She looked no older than nine. Her face was a strong contestant for the most good-looking one I'd seen so far here in *Infinite Dendrogram*. Of course, that was only among females. Rook was incontestably at the top if both genders were considered.

The girl in the photo had golden hair done into rolls and coils, and striking blue eyes that seemed to express a strength of heart. I also couldn't help but notice that her clothes were very well-made. I didn't know much about such apparel, but even I could tell that she wore a high-quality dress.

Her appearance, combined with the dignified way she was sitting in the chair, made the photo look like one of those formal marriage meeting photos.

She's a bit too young for that, though, I thought.

Anyway, there was no way I could've missed a person that stood out this much, so…

"I'm sorry, but I haven't seen her," I said. "So, who is she?"

From how the knights were panicking, I could only assume that she was the young lady of some important nobles.

"Eh?! Umm, uhh…" Liliana couldn't hide her surprise at my question and looked at me with a perplexed expression. It wasn't because she had trouble talking about the lady in the picture or anything. The bewilderment seemed too strong for that. She was acting as though I asked her something weird, like the answer to one plus one.

Once she realized that I really didn't know the girl, Liliana gave me the answer.

"This is the Kingdom of Altar's second princess, Elizabeth S. Altar."

"Ohhhhh." It all made sense now.

"When someone asks you something that's supposed to be common knowledge, it's only natural to become perplexed," commented Nemesis. "I'm not one to talk, though. Since we share most of our memories, I didn't know the girl, either."

How unbecoming of a Paladin, I thought of myself. I really should've investigated the ruling structure of the kingdom.

"So," I said. "If you're looking for her, then…"

"Her Highness went missing while we were visiting Gideon, and we of the Royal Guard are now searching for her," she explained.

This seems like some serious trouble, I thought.

Since I didn't know anything, Liliana gave me all the details about the disappearance of the princess.

First of all, she was the daughter of the king who had died in the war with Dryfe. The king had three daughters, but no sons. The missing girl's elder sister — the first princess — was the acting ruler of the country.

The Kingdom of Altar had no rule that prevented females from inheriting the throne, but historically, the country had had more kings than queens.

Due to that, even though a whole six months had passed since the fall of the king, the accession had yet to happen, and Elizabeth was still just "the second princess."

She had come here to Gideon to participate in some official event. She had arrived here and begun staying in Count Gideon's mansion about two days ago.

Yesterday, she had still been there to talk with the count and participate in the preparations for tomorrow's event. Today, she'd had plans to talk with some powerful people of this city. However, when one of Elizabeth's maids had gone to her room this morning, she found no sign of the princess anywhere.

There had been only a piece of paper — marked with the royal seal — that said "I will be back by evening." From the handwriting, it was clear that she hadn't been kidnapped, but had slipped out on her own volition.

Also, it was well known that the princess had wished to look around Gideon, and had become quite upset when she'd found out that she wasn't allowed to.

Additional info: Liliana made sure to be as indirect as possible when saying this, but the princess was whimsical, excessively vigorous, terribly insolent, and so full of curiosity that it was troubling.

Basically, the princess had slipped out of her roles just so she could go sightseeing in Gideon.

Of course, the Royal Guard couldn't just let her walk around the city by herself, so, naturally, they'd begun searching for her.

If there was one thing I could say to this situation...

"Don't you think you should up your security?" I asked.

I mean, they let this little girl slip past them. That's clearly not right.

"You are completely right about that..." she said.

But it turned out they'd actually had a valid excuse.

During the time period in which the princess had made her escape, there'd been a certain bit of trouble.

It had happened in the process of passing the role of protecting the princess from the Third Order of Knights to the Knights of the Royal Guard. It didn't seem like that could ever be particularly troublesome, but there had been a reason for it being so.

The princess' visit to this city had been planned a long time ago. Back then, it had been decided that her protection — from the moment she left the capital until she finished her business in Gideon and was safely back home — would be in the hands of the Royal Guard.

However, the player killer incident had made them postpone the day they'd left the capital.

Once the killers had been taken care of, they had finally been able to leave, but there had been a whole new problem. It was the event that — as we'd confirmed with our own eyes — had reduced Noz Forest to cinders.

Most assumed that the one responsible was King of Destruction the Unknown, but there was no proof of that.

However, it had to be known, so the role of meeting the King of Destruction and asking him about it had been given to the only one in the kingdom who knew him personally — Liliana. Apparently, everyone else who had been acquainted with him had died in the war.

Liliana was the Vice Commander of the Knights of the Royal Guard. However, since the Commander's seat was empty, she was basically the top of the order.

Since there were some problems with the prospect of the Royal Guard protecting the princess without Liliana's presence, the role had been hastily given to the Third Order of Knights. It had needed to be done because the princess' leave had already been belated due to the player killer incident, and they hadn't been able to afford any more delays. But that was the very cause of the trouble.

After she had finished questioning the King of Destruction about his role in the Noz Forest incident, Liliana and her Royal Guard had made their way to Gideon and arrived today, early in the morning. Right upon arriving, she had tried to take the role of protecting the princess from the Third Order of Knights.

During that process, both groups had looked at each others' documents and found out that there were some inconsistencies. The inconsistencies were so big, in fact, that no one could even believe that they'd actually happened.

They had all had to compare and adjust the documents they had while occasionally using magic communication tools to contact and confirm certain points with the people in the capital, and that had cost them more than an hour of time. Once they had finished that and mentally prepared themselves to protect Her Highness, they'd found out that the princess had disappeared.

"…Oh man," I said.

She had probably noticed the trouble going on and seen an opportunity to make her escape.

Sounds like she's a resourceful girl, I thought.

"The document trouble might've been devised by the princess," said Nemesis.

Ha ha ha, as if… I thought. Then I realized, *Wait, you know what? You might actually be right.*

Though it was slightly unrelated, Liliana's exchange with the King of Destruction had gone like so:

"Were you the one to do it?"

"YES."

"Why?"

"I was angry, so I just did it. I feel bad about it, though."

"I see. By the way, Noz Forest was a kingdom-owned lumbering ground. I would like you to pay to make up for all the wood you have burned. 130,000,000 lir, please.

"…Take it, you thief!"

"Oh, but I am an authority."

With that, the kingdom had instantly gotten enough money to function despite having lost Noz Forest. Apparently, it had helped them a lot.

I was mostly just surprised that people sitting at the top of the ranks could readily part with that much money.

"But man, he was just 'angry'...? What a troublesome guy," I said.

"Indeed," Liliana agreed. "Make sure to tell him off the next time you meet him."

"Eh? Ah... sure?" I didn't know how to respond.

What makes her think I have anything to do with him? I thought.

After telling me all the circumstances surrounding the princess' escape, Liliana ran off to search for her again.

She seemed to spend a lot of her time looking for people. I could only assume that she'd been born under that kind of star.

"Anyway, though it's a pretty big deal, the princess *merely* ran away," I said. "We just have to make sure to tell Liliana if we ever see the girl."

She hadn't been kidnapped or anything — she was just sightseeing. It didn't seem like it was something that could leave a bad taste in my mouth.

"I don't think you should be saying anything so careless," said Nemesis. "Try to consider your experiences so far. You seem to be some sort of event magnet. You get into all sorts of happenings, regardless of whether they're related to tians, monsters, or Masters."

...You might be right, I thought. *I haven't played the game for too long, yet I've experienced quite a lot.*

"I don't know how eventful other Masters' lives are, but don't you think that you're far above the average in that regard?" she asked.

Well, I *had* been thinking that my days here were pretty dense.

"If that knight girl was born under a star that led her into a life full of searching for people, you might've been born under a star of strife," said Nemesis. "I cannot recommend talking in a manner that could summon more such events."

"You're right," I said. "I'll keep that in mind."

All these exchanges had made me a bit hungry. Hunger was the reason we had come to this shop in the first place, so I began talking to the shopkeeper.

"Excuse me. Can we eat here?" I asked.

"Yes, certainly," he said. "We couldn't do any work until a few moments ago. We have to make up for the time lost."

"Oh yeah, you were questioned." I nodded. "Any specific reasons why?"

"Our shop is popular among young girls, so they probably assumed they could find a trace of the little lady here," he answered.

"Oh?" Nemesis reacted to something. "'Popular among young girls,' you say? Does that mean…?"

"Yes, we have a large selection of sweets," said the shopkeeper.

Nemesis' eyes lit up. "Excellent!" she cheered. "Master! Let's eat to our heart's content!"

"But I just bought some new gear," I said. "I'm not sure I want to use much more mon—"

"Two gacha pulls, 200,000 lir," she cut me off.

"I'm sorry. Please eat all you want," I said, giving in.

An hour later, Nemesis left the shop looking wholly satisfied after having eaten tons of sweets, while I walked out with my hands on my head as I despaired at the state of my inventory, which had less than 10,000 lir remaining.

That's too much… You ate way too much!

"And yet it still cost less than your gacha shenanigans," she said.

There was nothing I could say back to that.

"All right, I guess it's time to go outside and open up the capsule I pulled," I said.

"Indeed," Nemesis agreed. "I hope it's worth more than 200,000 lir."

...Yes, please, oh God almighty, I thought.

Once again, I went to the Nex Plains, where I'd tested my Miasmaflame Bracers. I distanced myself from Gideon's walls and stood in the grass several tens of meters away from the main road.

The capsule said, "Open only in spacious areas." I didn't know its standards for "spaciousness," but the place I was standing at was wide enough for an entire house or a ship to pop out without any problem.

"After all, I don't want to spawn something huge only to have it get stuck on the walls, destroy them, and get me into lots of trouble," I said.

"Time to open it, then?" asked Nemesis.

I took out the X capsule, twisted it to make it open, and caused something to pop out. It reminded me of that long-running game series where you grow monsters and have them fight other monsters.

"It's a..." I muttered.

I had been steeling myself for the appearance of something as large as a house or a ship, but the thing I'd gotten was nowhere near as big. In fact, it was even smaller than the shop employee's "carriage" example.

It wasn't too far off the mark, though. For what I had gotten was a horse. However, it didn't seem to be a living creature.

The horse was made of a silver-looking metal that was reminiscent of well-polished plate mail. Its shape was blatantly equestrian. It had been forged from what seemed to be armor pieces, and it had glimmering white orbs where its eyes were supposed to be. It could only be described as a "robot horse."

"So, it's not a monster?" asked Nemesis.

I seemed to be its official owner, and its description in my inventory went like so:

[Prism Steed, Zephyrus Silver]
[Special equipment: Mount]
One of the five Prism Steeds manufactured by Flagman — an artisan from an ancient civilization.
He who walks inside the wind.
[Details unknown.]

Details unknown? I raised an eyebrow. All the description had told me was that it was rideable and that it had a relation to the wind. With questioning eyes, I looked at both the window with the description and the Prism Steed, Zephyrus Silver — who I chose to call just "Silver."

Silver didn't seem to care, and only continued to stand in the field.

Upon further inspection, I noticed that his head didn't seem to have a mouth. The description said that he was *manufactured* by an artisan called Flagman, so it was obvious that he was a robot. However, he occasionally released sounds similar to neighs, kicked the ground with his hoof every now and then, and moved his fiber-made tail in a very horse-like manner.

The way it was impossible to tell which part of the sky he was looking at made him seem somewhat cat-like.

"How about riding him?" suggested Nemesis.

Good idea, I thought. Thankfully, Silver already had a saddle and reins, so I wouldn't have any problems getting on.

I closed in on him while being wary of kicks or something like that, but he turned out to be very obedient.

Once I took the reins, he lowered himself in a way that made his stomach partly touch the ground, making it easy for me to get on.

What a well-trained and friendly horse, I thought. It was strange that he was actually a robot.

I was quickly growing fond of him. I wanted to get on and speed through these fields on him.

After I sat down in the saddle, I placed my feet in the stirrups. After I did that, Silver stood up.

"Wow…" I murmured.

The view from atop of a horse was slightly moving. My visual point was much higher than when I stood on my own two feet, or when I'd ridden a pony when I was young.

Silver moved his hooves in a way that made it seem as though he wanted to dash through the fields right now.

"Be careful," warned Nemesis.

Riding together with Nemesis seemed pretty hard, so for now, I had her wait while I tried riding Silver by myself. I'd give her a chance to try after a short run.

"All right, let's go," I said. "Hi-yo, Silver! Away!"

Saying those words I've always wanted to say, I threw the reins, and at that moment, the sky and ground were reversed.

Unable to tell which way was really up, I felt as if I was falling upwards.

I could see Nemesis, who looked completely taken aback.

I could hear the sound of Silver running through the fields.

With my five senses in such a state, I fell to the ground — head first.

"Good thing it's just grass," Nemesis said that while looking down on me.

With my hand on top of my slightly creaking neck, I used healing magic on myself.

Silver was looking at me, and I couldn't tell whether he was worried or didn't think anything at all.

"I never would've expected you to fall off on the very first step," said Nemesis.

Same here, I thought. I'd fallen off the very moment Silver had begun to run.

"You had a small audience looking at you from the main road," said Nemesis. "They all made expressions much like mine when they saw what happened."

That seemed like an appropriate reaction, honestly.

"...Why did that happen, though?" I couldn't help but ask. I hadn't been riding him in a weird way or anything. The way I'd been thrown off seemed to ignore all laws of physics.

"It's a wonder, indeed," Nemesis agreed. "You're a Paladin, so you should be able to ride horses without any problems."

"Exactly, so... hm?" Realizing something, I took a look at Silver's skills. There was a total of three — Running, Wind Hoof, and one unknown skill that said "????," just like a skill on the Miasmaflame Bracers.

I took a look at the details of the "Running" skill.

Allows running while someone is riding. The rider must have either Horse Riding or Riding skills.

"Horse Riding... skill?" I read out loud.

I can't ride Silver without that skill? I thought. *I can only make him walk around?*

"Well, you don't have the skill," said Nemesis. "Strange, considering that you're a Paladin."

"There aren't many skills I can learn from my job," I said. The only ones I had so far were Paladin's Aegis and the low-tier healing magic.

"Strange," she seemed puzzled. "A Paladin is basically an upgrade to Knight, so you have every reason to have the Horse Riding skill."

"Yeah," I agreed. "…Wait, an upgrade?"

Wait, Paladins were upgraded Knights.

The realization of the implications made me break out in a cold sweat.

"Nemesis, I'm going offline for a second."

"Hm? W-Well, if you insist…"

After logging out, I went on my PC and began doing research on the Horse Riding skill and the relationship between low-rank and high-rank jobs.

Horse Riding was a skill that practically represented the Knight — the low-rank job that usually came before Paladin. Therefore, anyone who took the normal path and became a Paladin after having been a Knight would naturally have the Horse Riding skill. But, due to some twists of fate, I'd ended up skipping Knight and going straight to Paladin.

Doing so had given me a great stat growth and a head start over most newbies. However, the number of skills the Paladin job had given me was really lacking. In fact, I only had a mere two — Paladin's Aegis and First Heal.

Rook had far more, as a Pimp — a low-rank job. I could only assume that skills from high-rank jobs required the player to learn skills from low-rank jobs of the same grouping.

According to the walkthrough wiki, Knights had no access to Paladin's Aegis or any healing spells — they could only be learned after becoming a Paladin. Other skills that could be learned by Paladin were Grand Cross — which was considered to be the job's ultimate attack — and Purifying Silverlight — which no one really knew how to get.

All skills except for these four were extensions of skills learned by Knights. That included offensive and other skills... such as Horse Riding.

I sat at my PC and silently processed the facts.

I didn't have a single offensive Paladin skill. My level was in the mid-20s. I definitely should've had one by now. But I didn't, which meant that my assumption was correct.

Most Paladin skills required the player to learn the skills from the low-rank job of the same grouping — Knight.

Why didn't my brother warn me about this? I thought. *...Oh, I guess he just didn't know anyone who'd started with a high-rank job, so my case was a first to him.*

I had a feeling that — like Rook's Lost Heart — many high-rank jobs required the person to have reached the max level on low-rank jobs of the same grouping. Even Paladin requirements weren't ones that could be fulfilled by your standard level 0 newbies, so it was natural for him not to know about this.

"...I see," I muttered. It all made sense now. I couldn't learn the skill and ride Silver without switching to the low-rank job, Knight.

I didn't care much about the offensive skills. I had Nemesis with me, and I'd recently gotten my hands on the Miasmaflame Bracers. However, to ride Silver, I had to find a way to learn the Horse Riding skill.

I searched around for a way to learn it without switching to Knight, and it didn't take long for me to find it.

There was an accessory called "Amulet of the Equestrian Tribe," which gave a +1 to the Horse Riding skill. That was the only thing I would need to be able to ride Silver.

That wasn't all. Jobs which had the aptitude for skills acquired through accessory effects could actually master those skills and make them their own. Since Paladin was an upgrade to Knight, it was obvious that I had the aptitude for Horse Riding.

"Yes! This is it!" I exclaimed.

Quickly concluding that I had to go to Gideon's marketplace and buy one of those accessories, I took a look at how much they went for.

Amulet of the Equestrian Tribe — Market Price: 100,000 lir.

I fell to the ground.

"We *have* to find ways to get money." I logged back in and stated our next course of action.

"Well, we have less than 10,000 lir left," Nemesis nodded. "We would've had to get money even if we didn't have this problem with Silver."

She was right. We were nearly broke, so we had to do something about it regardless.

I seem to have a knack for getting big money and quickly losing it all, I thought. *Strange, considering that I'm not actually wasting it.*

"Gacha," said Nemesis.

A-Again, I-I'm not actually wasting it.

"By the way, unlike the first Permit, the second one wasn't signed, right?" she said. "Why did you just give it to Rook instead of selling it? I can't be sure if you would've gotten the 100,000 lir you spent on it, but you could've received at least half of that, no?"

"...Ah," I said. She had a point.

"You..." Nemesis couldn't find the words to express what she felt.

"No, it's fine," I said. "I already gave it to Rook. A man does not go back on his word. We'll find other ways to make money."

"That's easy to say," she said. "However, Rook is currently offline and asleep, while Miss Sunglasses has her hands full with some other business. There's a limit to how much we can do just by ourselves."

"Yep, that's a bit of a problem," I agreed. I could go and accept some quest, but since I was solo, my choices were limited to the ones with low difficulty and thus low rewards.

There was also the meeting we had planned for tomorrow afternoon, so I couldn't take any quests that would last too long.

"Perhaps we should hunt for a bounty? Like that demon?" suggested Nemesis.

"That'll get us a death penalty if we fail, though," I said. "We wouldn't make it for tomorrow's arrangement."

"I see this world just isn't nice enough to give us a means of getting 100,000 lir in a short amount of time," she said.

Time wasn't a big problem — I'd have had tons of it after the surprise Marie had in store for us tomorrow. However, I wanted to ride Silver as soon as possible.

"What about the arena, then?" asked Nemesis. "It allows fighting without the risk of death penalty and rewards the victor, no?"

"Yeah, well, I looked it up and found out that you can only participate when your total level is above 51," I answered.

During the testing this morning, my level had gone up to 26. I still had a way to go before the arena was open to me.

"Oh, yeah!" Something came to me. "I can still bet on the fighters! I'll put my money on who I think will win and—"

"Don't," Nemesis cut me off. "Fortune might favor you when it really counts, but most of the time, you're just plain unlucky."

…*You're not wrong there,* I thought.

"Guess I'll have to give up on getting the Amulet of the Equestrian Tribe by today or tomorrow and just do some basic money-making instead," I sighed.

"Good idea," Nemesis agreed. "With that in mind, let's make our way to the Adventurers' Guild."

Nemesis and I began walking towards Gideon's first district, where the guild building was.

"By the way," Nemesis spoke up again. "I know that borrowing from Rook isn't an option, but what about Brother Bear?"

"Having him lend me money would make me feel like a loser," I said.

"Hmm…" she pondered. "What about your old equipme—"

"Already sold it," I answered before she could finish. *And all the earnings I got from it have disappeared into your endless stomach,* I thought.

The only property I owned currently was the gear I was wearing and the less than 10,000 lir I had remaining.

"Oh, this talk about equipment reminds me..." said Nemesis. "Why are you so averse to glasses?"

"...What?" I asked.

"I've been wondering about it since our exchange with the penguin," she continued. "I tried looking through your memories, but I couldn't do it because it's in the deepest, most private section of all. Honestly, the defenses on it are way too strong, and I can't help but wonder why."

...That seems like a strong sign that I don't want to talk about it and that you shouldn't be asking me this, I thought. *But okay, I'll talk.* Nemesis and I were basically one and the same, so there should be no harm in telling her.

"Back when I was a kid," I said, "my eyesight was very poor. When I got into year 4 of elementary school, I happened to be the only kid in class who wore glasses."

"Well, things like that happen every now and then," Nemesis commented.

"My nickname instantly became 'Noby,' like the character from *Doraemon*," I continued.

"...Hm?" she raised an eyebrow.

"My classmates used 'Noby' more than my real name," I went on. "They often pressed me to say his trademark *Doraemon* phrase, even though I didn't sound much like the character. Not only that, but the theme of the school's arts festival somehow became *Doraemon*, and, of course, I was given the role of Noby."

It wasn't like I had been bullied. Nor had I been some sort of outcast. In fact, I'd had a lot of friends. My classmates at that time had clearly had no ill will, and had only given me the nickname because we were somewhat close. However, the lack of a proper outlet had made a certain sentiment grow within me.

It could basically be summed up with the words "Who are you calling 'Noby'?" Or, "I love *Doraemon* and all, but this is a completely different matter."

Nemesis was silently staring at me.

"What wrong, Nemesis?" I asked her.

"The reason is just so trifling that I don't know how to react," she answered.

"...Well, even I know that it's not such a big deal," I admitted. My big sister had reacted the same way when I'd told her about it.

"You said you had poor eyesight," Nemesis spoke again. "Do you still wear glasses in real life?"

"No," I answered. "My vision was corrected over the course of the five years after the school's arts festival."

I had eaten things that were good for my eyes and trained them by looking far ahead and by moving my eyeballs daily. It'd been hard work.

"I admire your tenacity, but wouldn't it have been better to just get contact lenses?" she asked.

"The idea of putting things in my eyes scares me," I answered.

"Master, you..." She was completely out of things to say.

"Naturally, laser eye surgery scared me, too, so I had to fix my eyesight with steady training and... Hm?"

As Nemesis and I were walking through the streets and chatting, I suddenly heard some unpleasant sounds coming from a nearby back alley.

They made me curious, so I went towards their source.

A short distance away from the main road, between the buildings, there was a slightly larger area where I saw five men encircling a single girl.

The men looked like the most stereotypical, run-of-the-mill, boorish punks. The sight reminded me of what Liliana had told me about the princess who'd run away, which had made me picture a generic scenario where I encountered her being harassed by a bunch of evil bastards. Thinking that it couldn't be the case, I took a better look at the scene, and... it actually wasn't.

The damsel in distress had a decent appearance, but her facial features were definitely those of a commoner. She wouldn't have seemed out of place if I'd seen her standing outside a restaurant and attracting customers. The girl definitely wasn't the princess, but that didn't matter, considering how much trouble she was in.

The contents of their exchange could be summed up like so:

The girl had a little brother who had been kidnapped yesterday.

These men had blackmailed her, saying that she had to prepare 200,000 lir if she wanted him back. They had also added that her brother would be killed if she told anything to the knights.

The girl had run around, borrowing money and selling their family's possessions until she'd barely managed to gather the 200,000 lir. She had then brought the ransom money to the place the kidnappers had named — this back alley — and given it to them.

The men had readily accepted the money, but they'd had absolutely no intention of giving her little brother back. Not only that — they were about to take the girl herself as an extra.

Well, damn, I thought. *They're scumbags to the core.*

They were tians, not monsters — at least not in the game sense — but it was clear that kicking their asses wouldn't give me any pangs of conscience.

And letting it slide would leave a bad taste in my mouth.

With that thought, I stood up and showed myself to the scumbags.

"Stop right there!" I exclaimed and instantly realized that my voice was doubled for some reason.

"...Hm?" I said in surprise, and it happened once again.

Okay, what the hell? I thought.

I'd done nothing special — I'd merely jumped out and said something — but my voice had come out as if it was in-sync with another one.

A moment later, I noticed the cause. There was another person standing behind the scumbags and the girl — at the other side of the back alley.

It was a young man who looked about as old as I was and had donned some strangely-designed clothing that seemed to be a mix of a military uniform and a rider suit. The gloves he wore exposed the backs of his hands, and the left one had a crest which made it obvious that he was a Master.

"It matters not," he said. "Back away from that fair lady, you vile scoundrels."

Apparently, he was just a guy who'd happened to be thinking the exact same thing I had been thinking at the exact same time.

"P-Please, help!" pled the girl.

"Heh," he grinned. "Why, certainly. All beauteous flowers have thorns. And it is my mission in life to be the thorn for ladies as lovely as yourself and to sting any ruffians trying to harm you."

Though we seemed to be alike in some ways, I wasn't nearly as pompous as him. The aura around him almost made me imagine roses and unnatural rays of light like in some manga aimed at young girls or a Takarazuka Revue performance.

"Who the hell are you two?" demanded one of the scumbags.

Another got excited. "Huh? Ya wanna go? Let's do this!"

"Hyahaah!" one just cheered in a discomforting way.

"There's five of us, ya dumb shits!" spoke yet another.

"That's two times more than you!" the last one added.

That's not two times, you numbskull, I thought. *It's 2.5 times.*

"Heh," the pompous Master grinned. "Indeed, there are more of you, but what are your levels?"

"Huh?!" One of them got scared.

"From what I can tell, you are all on your first low-rank job," said the pompous weirdo. "*My* total level, however, is 126."

"W-What?!" They all freaked out in unison.

"Heh," he grinned yet again. "Now, bear witness to my power. I'll just summon my Garage and…"

"Get him before he does anything!" shouted one of the scumbags. The other four let out a battle cry and charged at him.

"What?!" the guy was surprised. "Wait, I need to get in my Magingear and… No matter! I will do this with my bare hands if I must!"

I felt as though I was reading a delinquent manga. All five of the hoodlums ran towards the guy in the military uniform with their fists ready to strike.

And so, due to just how much the weirdo was standing out, I was being completely ignored.

"Oh well," I sighed. The timing was good, so I spoke to the girl. "You should run away now."

"Th-Thank you very much!" She thanked me with palpable fear in her voice and ran to the street behind me.

"Okay, that's done," I said. "And the battle is… wait, what?"

I looked to the other side and — to my surprise — saw the guy in the uniform getting beaten to a pulp. The five hoodlums weren't unharmed or anything, but it was still safe to say that the battle was completely one-sided.

Seems like there are too many of them for him to take on by himself, I thought. *But wait, his total level is 126, so how… Oh, I see.*

"Having a high total level doesn't mean that you have high stats, as well," I said aloud. He was probably like Rook, who — due to being a Pimp — had half of most of my stats despite his level being two times greater than mine.

Nonetheless, 126 was a formidable level. If the five scumbags were taking care of him *that* easily, it was entirely possible that I wouldn't fare so well, either.

As that thought went through my head, one of the five raised his fist and charged towards me. "You're next!"

I hastily evaded his attack and countered with a punch directed straight into his face.

The next moment, the man got blasted away to the other side of the alley.

"…Eh?" The other four hoodlums were shocked.

"…Why?" I asked, as perplexed as the scumbags.

Thinking that Nemesis had done something, I turned around and looked at her. She responded by heaving a light sigh and pointing at the back of her hand. That action made me look at the backs of my own hands and reminded me of a certain fact.

I was wearing the Miasmaflame Bracers.

While testing them today, I had focused mainly on their ability to release fire and gas, but those weren't the only features they had. The item could also be used for defense and gave a bonus to my stats. Specifically, it increased my STR by 100%.

Back when I had been level 0, my STR had been somewhere around 10. I hadn't had any problems moving my body back then, so I could only assume that that amount was representative of a standard adult male's strength. I'd leveled up and increased my stats since then, and with the bonus from Miasmaflame Bracers, my STR was now over 400. That meant that I'd just punched a hoodlum in the face with the strength of more than 40 average adult males.

"Is he dead?" Slightly worried, I took a look at the guy, who was lying on the other side of the alley.

He was twitching, so it was safe to assume that he'd survived. I heaved a sigh of relief. It was pretty obvious that their jobs were combat-oriented, so they were probably tougher than the average Joe.

"It's all good, then," I said as I closed in on them while bashing my bracers together.

The results wouldn't have been pretty if I'd used Nemesis, so I chose to settle it with the bad boys on my hands.

"Who's next?" I asked.

"Eee!" one of them shrieked like a little girl.

I probably looked a bit too menacing, since they quickly turned pale, whirled around, and ran away like roaches.

"D-Damn it!" one of them shouted. "Don't get cocky, you shits! We still have that bitch's brother!" With that, they disappeared into the main road.

Man, what a generic set of scumbags, I thought.

"Are you okay?" I asked. "First Heal."

I walked over to the uniformed guy they'd beaten up and cast my healing spell on him.

His wounds weren't deep by any stretch of the imagination, and my basic healing magic quickly closed them all.

"Heh, thank you," he said gratefully. "Hm? Those ears are..." He looked up at the things on my head — the dog ears I'd grown because of the mad penguin.

"What about them?" I asked.

"...Oh, nothing," he answered. "It's a nice accessory."

"Find a penguin and you can get your own pair," I said.

"Heh." He grinned yet again. "I will keep that in mind."

The man stood up and dusted his clothes. Even that action seemed a bit pompous.

"I feel that this meeting is fated," he said. "Allow me to introduce myself. My name is Hugo Lesseps. I am a Master and my job is High Pilot."

"I'm Ray Starling," I responded. "I'm a Master and a Paladin. And this is my Embryo, Nemesis."

"I see... Embryos of the Maiden type are quite a rarity," he said. "It's a pleasure to meet such a lovely mademoiselle."

"Pleased to meet you, too," said Nemesis.

I found it interesting that he could tell that Nemesis was a Maiden and not a Guardian just by looking at her.

But man, the way he talks sounds like it belongs in a play or something, I thought. *I wonder where he's from. If his name is anything to go by, then he's probably French.*

"By the way, why did they beat you up so easily?" I asked. "Is your job not battle-oriented or something?" They'd been pretty weak when I'd fought them, so I would've assumed that someone with a total level of 126 could've handled them easily.

"Heh." There was that grin again. "I am a level 50 Pilot, level 50 Mechanic, and level 26 High Pilot. Leveling with these jobs only raises my HP, MP, SP, and DEX, so all my other stats are about what they were when I started out!"

That didn't seem like something to be proud of. Also, I couldn't help but wonder just what kind of jobs they were to have such a biased stat growth.

Does he drive a car or something? I thought. *Is he like a character from* Metal Max *or something?*

"U-Umm…" I said.

As I pondered the nature of Hugo's job, someone called out to me.

I turned around to see the girl we'd helped out. Apparently, she'd chosen to stay nearby instead of running away completely.

"Th-Thank you very much for helping me!" she cried.

"Oh, no need for that," I said. "I did it because I felt like it." Also, it would've left a bad taste in my mouth if I hadn't.

"Heh." Hugo grinned again. "I feel the same way. I don't know if I could sleep at night after having ignored a lady in distress."

Isn't that much like my go-to phrase for these situations? I thought.

"U-Umm… Are you Masters?" the girl ventured.

"Why, yes," said Hugo. "Myself and Ray here are both Masters."

The girl dropped to the ground before us and pushed her head against it.

"Lady…" Hugo didn't seem sure how to react. "Please raise your head."

"Please… Please save my little brother!" she pled. "I beg of you!"

Oh, yeah, the scumbags said something about that while running away, I thought.

"Save him? As in, from those hoodlums?" I asked.

"Y-Yes!" she said. "They're the Gouz-Maise Gang… They kidnap children, and if they don't get the ransom for them, the boys and girls get killed and e-eate— ohhh…"

Her words made me turn silent.

Killing and eating children? I thought in disbelief. *Ohhh, man…*

"They kidnapped my little brother, so please, save him!" she exclaimed. "I can give you this money! And if that's not enough, I'll do whatever you want…"

She extended the bag with the ransom towards us and begged while crying her eyes out.

I knew the circumstances from the eavesdropping I'd done before jumping out to help her. As things were, her brother would've been killed and eaten sooner rather than later. To prevent that result from becoming reality, one had to act fast, and the only ones who could do that were Hugo and me.

Honestly, I had a feeling it would come to this the moment I showed myself to the scumbags, I thought. *That's why I'm fully prepared to face the risks.*

"I'm down for it," I said. "I don't need any compensation, though."

91

"B-But…"

"You went through great lengths to gather this ransom money, right?" I said. "I can't take it." I had a feeling that I would've done something about it even if she hadn't asked me to. If I'd ignored it, the aftertaste in my mouth would've been downright foul.

"What about you, Hugo?" I asked.

"Heh," he grinned. "A foolish question. *Of course* I'm doing it. And I don't need any money, either."

Hugo went down on one of his knees, gently placed his left hand on her chin, and made her look upwards. He then gently wiped her tears away with the thumb of his right hand.

"Lady," he said gently. "We shall stop your tears." And so — as if acting out a scene from a play — Hugo smiled at her. "I promise that you will greet tomorrow's morning with a smile on your face."

[The quest "Rescue Roddie Lancarse, Difficulty Level 8" has started]
[Please see the quest window for further details]

A message directed to my ears announced the beginning of an event quest. Apparently, the same thing had happened to Hugo.

"Let us go, Ray," he said. "The mission awaits."

"Okay," I sighed. "I can dance to this tune of yours." Our target quest was the difficulty level 8 "Rescue Roddie Lancarse." Our destination was the hideout of man-eaters and kidnappers — the Gouz-Maise Gang.

Our goal… was a morning of smiles.

And so, we began our quest.

Chapter Three 》 A Maiden's Master

Gideon, the city of duels, Paladin Ray Starling

Nemesis, Hugo, and I got on a difficulty level 8 random event quest called "Rescue Roddie Lancarse." Just like the quest to save Milianne, it was going to be a race against time. However, I had two other worries about it.

First was the quest difficulty. I didn't know just how difficult level 8 quests were, so I asked Hugo about it…

"Difficult enough for level 500 tians going solo to fail spectacularly," he said. "Even a full party of such tians would have a hard time."

…and that was his answer. So, level 8 quests were too difficult for max level tians. Even if we Masters were generally stronger than tians, it was clearly a bit too much for me — someone below level 50 — to handle. However, I had no intention of leaving the child for dead just because it was hard to save him.

"I must say that letting them escape was a grave mistake," said Nemesis.

And that was my other worry — the five scumbags we'd faced.

The one I'd punched was still spread out on the back alley's pavement, so Hugo tied him up with a wire he had on him. We decided to hand him over to the guards, so the girl we'd helped — Rebecca — ran off to the guardroom.

The other four had run away with a threat regarding her brother, unfortunately. We didn't know where their base was. If they got there before us and told everyone about what happened here, the boy's life would be in more danger than ever.

"Man, I should've gassed them," I said. A whiff of the poison from my Miasmaflame Bracers would've rendered them completely immobile.

"We're in the city, so wouldn't that count as terrorism?" asked Nemesis.

You have a point, I thought. *Although I could've also scorched their legs with fire from the left bracer and make them unable to walk, and...*

"I can tell that you're thinking something disturbing," said Hugo. "Let me assure you, though, that there's no need to worry about them." He then pointed to the street they'd run off to.

I couldn't see what was behind the corner, but I could hear something being dragged on the ground.

"What's that sound?" I asked. The source got closer and closer until it soon entered my vision.

"Shorry for the waith, Hugo." It was a girl. If you ignored the ushanka hat on her head, she would've been about as tall as Nemesis.

The first thing I noticed about her was her *whiteness*. White hair, white cheeks, white hat. Despite it not being particularly cold, she also wore a white felt long coat and a white scarf. And, for some reason, she was also biting into a white manju sweet. The only non-white thing about her were her blue eyes.

"Heh." Hugo turned pompous again. "Well done, Cyco."

She gulped down the manju before responding. "It's a pain, but they were weak, so don't mind it."

I looked down and saw that she was holding people — the four hoodlums that had escaped — by the clothes behind the napes of their necks.

The ease with which she was holding two people in each hand clearly didn't fit her appearance, but I soon noticed the Master crest on her left hand.

Well, I guess her strength makes sense if she's a Master, I thought.

The way she spoke was extremely monotone, and I couldn't tell if she was role-playing or if that was her normal way of speaking.

She noticed me examining her and shot a glare at Nemesis and me. "Hugo the girl pamperer befriended a lolicon? You like little girls, mister?"

"Who are you calling a lolicon?!" I shouted.

"Who are you calling a loli?!" Nemesis howled at the same time.

She actually marked me as a sexual deviant with her first words to me! Who the hell does that?! I thought.

"That flat chest and low height are exemplary loli features," she said. "And anyone who has a loli service him is a real lolicon."

Slander if I'd ever heard any. Nemesis was a part of me, so she didn't count.

"No!" said Nemesis. "This form of mine merely prioritizes beauty over function!"

"A Master with an Embryo who claims *that* form to be beauty is a lolicon to the core," said the white girl.

"You little…! Seems like I have to do something about that mouth of yours!" Nemesis shouted.

"Try it."

Nemesis jumped on the girl, who faced her head-on, as emotionless as ever. They began fighting, but I felt like I was watching two cats mess about.

It sure is rare for Nemesis to be this honest with anyone that's not me, I thought.

"So, Hugo," I spoke up. "Who is this monotone and monochrome girl who has no qualms about labeling strangers as perverts?"

"Cyco," he answered. "She's my… party member. I contacted and told her to catch the ones that ran away. The girl's a bit foul-mouthed, yes, but as you can see, she's quite reliable. Oh, and just so you're aware, the things she just said are far from the worst you can hear from her."

"Seriously?" I raised an eyebrow.

"Yes," he nodded. "Especially when compared to the abuse she spouts at our clan owner."

…I don't think I can even imagine that, I thought.

Well, her foul mouth aside, we now had a total of three Masters in our party. Naturally, that increased our chances of successfully completing the quest.

"All right, Cyco, tell us what you found out," said Hugo.

"Okay," Cyco replied while her hands were fixed with Nemesis' as they pushed each other in what seemed like a situation straight out of a pro wrestling match. Still in that state, she turned her face to Hugo and began talking. "After I beat up and interrogated them, they told me where their hideout was. It's beyond the east gate, in the Cruella Mountain Belt. The specific location was in a map they had."

Skillfully using her mouth, she bit into a paper she had in a pocket on her side and threw it over to Hugo using only her head.

"Cruella Mountain Belt?" I repeated the place name. It was an area I hadn't been in before.

"That's the name of the mountains to the east of this city," said Hugo. "The area beyond them is Caldina's territory."

"So it's basically the border between the two countries," I said.

"It's a great place for a bandit hideout," he continued. "Any Kingdom of Altar military operations done in the Cruella Mountain Belt would be taken as acts of war against Caldina."

"Why don't the two countries team up to take care of the bandits, then?" I asked. Bandits lurking near the border seemed like a big problem for both Altar and Caldina, so it would've been natural to team up and exterminate them.

"That will never happen," said Hugo. "Caldina only acts when there's money to be had. In fact, they would do *anything* for it."

"By that, you mean…?" I asked.

"For the right price, the vilest bandit could be a valued customer."

So they're in on this? I thought.

"I would guess they get paid a lot and provide passive cooperation in exchange," he continued. "Caldina probably agreed to react in some way if the kingdom's army made a move. Even if it was all just an act, the kingdom still couldn't do what they wanted."

Hugo opened the map that Cyco had given him. On the left side of it was Gideon. The right portrayed a desert, and the area right in the middle of them had several mountains. The second closest mountain to Gideon had a circle marking something.

"This is the place," said Hugo. "It's beyond a mountain. Seems like we'll have to make haste."

"Yeah," I agreed. "We'll have to run real fast."

For some reason, Hugo gave me a strange look.

"What?" I asked.

"Ray," he said. "You're a Paladin, aren't you? Won't you be riding a mount?"

"I have a horse, but I can't ride it because I don't have the Horse Riding skill," I answered.

"So that's how it is…" he said, looking completely weirded out.

"…Yeah."

Well, this is awkward, I thought.

"Heh," he chuckled. "This is the first time I'm seeing anyone who doesn't have the Horse Riding skill while being in the knight grouping."

"Is it normal for us to have it?" I asked.

"Well," Hugo said. "Let's just say that I feel as though someone just told me that they're a swimmer, but can't do the front crawl, backstroke, breaststroke, or butterfly stroke."

"Is there even anything more to swimming than those four?" I asked.

"The dog paddle and traditional Japanese swimming?" he suggested.

Those didn't seem like they fit.

"Anyway, I see how it is," said Hugo. "Leave it to me. I have a means of travel that allows us to get to their hideout in a short amount of time."

"Thanks," I said gratefully.

In unrelated news, Nemesis and Cyco had become friends during the fight, and were now exchanging a firm handshake.

Friendship is a great thing, I thought. *But man, the fact that one is black and the other's white reminds me of a girl's anime from a few decades back.*

Our party — Hugo, Cyco, and me with Nemesis as my blade — had made our way through the eastern gate in Gideon's third district and were now standing before the entrance to the Cruella Mountain Belt area.

There was a road leading towards the mountains, which was being used by carriages and the like.

We were about to make our way to the gang's hideout by using the means of travel Hugo mentioned, but...

"What *is* that means of travel, anyway?" I asked.

"This isn't the right place for it," he said. "We have to go where there are even fewer people."

He can't show it to anyone or something? I thought. "Does it stand out or something?"

"You could say that, yes," he answered.

And so we walked for about fifteen minutes. We weren't following the road, either. Hugo actually led us into some forest.

All right, this is weird, I thought. We were nowhere close to any proper road that could be used by carriages and such.

If we were about to use something rideable, the mountain road near Gideon would have been much better for it.

"This place seems good," he said upon discovering an opening in the forest. It was circular and had a radius of about ten meters. There was a curious lack of tall trees, and it seemed like the plants here had only just begun sprouting.

"My guess is that someone with a magic-based job used an area-of-effect offensive spell here," said Hugo. "I don't know how it was for those affected, but it's convenient for us."

He reached into his inventory, took out a silver sheet, and spread it out on the ground.

Once he did that, I realized just how big the sheet was. It was a square with sides that were about five meters in size.

"I've prepared the Garage," said Hugo. "Cyco, any hostiles nearby?"

"None at all," she answered. "I'm not picking up any monsters or people."

"Roger that." Hugo opened a window and began doing something on it. A moment later, sounds of machinery began coming out from under the sheet he'd spread on the ground.

"…Wait, machinery?" I muttered. Suddenly, I realized something.

Hugo's job was High Pilot. The noun "pilot" was generally used on people who operated something mechanical. However, this world didn't have any machinery that could be "driven" in that sense…

…unless it was related to a certain country.

"Hugo," I said. "You're…"

"Ray," he spoke up before I could finish. "I am taking part in this quest as a *person* and as a thorn protecting the beautiful flowers we call 'women.'"

His statement made it obvious that he'd known exactly what I was gonna say.

"Why are *you* on this quest?" he continued. "Is it because you're a Paladin of the kingdom, or because you're your own man?"

There was only one thing I could say in response.

"Ignoring this would leave a bad taste in my mouth." It was the exact same thing I'd thought when I accepted this quest. "At the very least, I'm not doing this because of my occupation."

"Nor am I." With those words, Hugo gave a wry smile and pushed down on a button on the window. It said "sortie" on it.

Right after that, the sheet on the ground began to expand. Its surface began to slip and open up like a garage shutter, exposing a cavity that completely ignored the sheet's thickness.

Four pillars rose up at the corners of the sheet and stopped when they were about five meters tall.

A moment later, a roaring sound came from the bottom of the cavity as a lift began rising up until it reached the surface.

On it, there was a large object. Its two arms and legs gave it a humanoid appearance. However, it was nowhere near human.

It was about six heads tall, but its height was above five meters and it was covered in a dark green steel coating.

On its pelvic area, there was a gun and an army knife that fit its great size, and it didn't seem like that was the extent of the weaponry it had in store.

Its chest area was open, and inside, I saw a cockpit that bore a striking resemblance to one I had seen in some old anime.

In conclusion, it was a humanoid battle robot.

"'Magic and Gear,'" he said. "More widely known as Magingear. The main weapon of the Dryfe Imperium."

Hugo — a High Pilot of the Dryfe Imperium — said that as he got into the cockpit.

"...Hugo," I said, impressed.

"Right now, I am but a knight fighting for a lady's tears," he told me. "You are not a Paladin of the Kingdom of Altar, either. Am I correct, fellow knight?"

"...Yeah," I nodded.

Yet again, he'd donned that aura straight out of a young girls' manga or a Takarazuka performance and spoken as if he were a character from a play. Despite how ridiculous it seemed, I couldn't help but agree with what he'd said.

The Kingdom and the Imperium had been at war once. There was a ceasefire going on right now, but it was rumored that it was going to get heated again within the next few months. The countries we served were true enemies.

However, as we were right now, that didn't matter to us. It was also completely irrelevant to the girl who'd cried for her brother and the boy we were going to save.

Our standings had absolutely no connection to what we had to do. When we'd taken this quest, we had been acting as our own individual human beings.

"Shall we go?" he asked from his cockpit.

"We shall," I answered and jumped on the hand of the Magingear he was piloting. The other hand was already occupied by Cyco.

With both its hands full, Hugo's Magingear stood up.

"Demi-Dragon-tier Magingear, Marshall II... Sortie!"

And so, the Marshall II began dashing towards our goal — the other side of the mountain.

Magingear. That was the abbreviation of "Magic and Gear" — a term used to describe the imperium's main type of weapon.

As I sat on this weapon's right hand, all the shaking caused by its running made me think of something.

The first Embryo I'd seen after beginning to play *Infinite Dendrogram* had been my brother's Baldr. That was a technological weapon, too, but since it was an Embryo — something that was unique to each Master — it wasn't quite the same as something made by technology.

The Magingear, however, were weapons born from Dryfe Imperium's scientific prowess — a part of the world's setting.

As far as I was aware, the imperium was the only country in *Infinite Dendrogram* that excelled in technology and science. That fact made me curious as to why the other countries didn't follow its footsteps.

Technological innovation was something that would normally spread like wildfire. The imperium had been a technological nation for more than a hundred years. Reason suggested that their knowledge should've spread to other countries by now.

When you looked at it as a game, it was probably safe to say that the reason was that the developers wanted to keep each country unique. However, *Infinite Dendrogram's* setting was detailed enough to incorporate the basic function of logging in and out. That made me think that the technological gap between the nations wasn't without a world-building reason, too.

So, as we made our way to the hideout of the Gouz-Maise Gang, I asked Hugo about it. "What do you think?"

"Heh," he grinned. "To know the answer to that, you have to know about a certain civilization."

"Civilization?" I repeated.

"Yes," said Hugo. "It's called either the 'lost' or the 'ancient' civilization."

...That name seems familiar, I thought. *Oh, right. Silver — the horse I pulled from the gacha — had "ancient civilization" in his description.*

"That civilization existed a few thousand years ago," Hugo continued.

According to Hugo, the ancient civilization had been highly advanced in terms of technology. It was similar to the imperium in that regard, but their technology had been superior to anything Dryfe had now.

However, the civilization perished, leaving behind only a few machines and texts that archeologists stumbled upon every now and then.

"You're gonna have to tell me more than that," I said.

"There are theories that the grand civilization disappeared because their technological advancement made the people too arrogant, and therefore it incurred some divine wrath," he explained. "According to the legends, a god and his thirteen servants went around destroying every civilization that existed back then. Every country besides Dryfe and Granvaloa believes that legend, so the people *choose* not to make any scientific and technological advancements."

I see, I thought. *So they're actively avoiding technology because they're afraid of divine punishment. Hm...? Dryfe and Granvaloa?*

"That doesn't apply to those two countries, then?" I asked. "And wait, Granvaloa is scientifically advanced?"

"Well..." he said and pondered. "You might say that Granvaloa has science and you might say that it doesn't."

How am I supposed to process that?

"First, let me tell you about Dryfe," he said. "Dryfe has always presented itself as the true successors of the ancient civilization and thus didn't shy away from technology and science. However, all their attempts to recreate the technology of the ancient times have failed, so they had to compromise for machines such as the Magingear, which only functioned by using people's magic.

"People's magic?" I asked.

"Yes, they can only move at the cost of MP. Right now, my Marshall II uses 1MP per minute. In battle, it would be 1MP per second. There are differences in extent, but this is how every Dryfe machine works."

MP per second, eh? Reminds me of my Reversal, I thought.

Anyway, a certain thing made sense now. *That* was the reason why Hugo's jobs — Pilot, Mechanic, and High Pilot — were so focused on MP growth.

"So the machines of the past were different?" I asked.

"Many of the ones that have been excavated had generators installed in them," he answered. "They provided the machines with all the magic they needed to operate, and as far as I'm aware, they're a technology lost to the modern world."

Interesting, I thought. *I wonder where Silver stands in all of this.*

"Can you expand on Granvaloa?" I asked. "I didn't know that they had machine technology." All I knew about it was that it was a country on the sea, so I had always imagined it functioned with sail-based ships, like the ones in the Age of Discovery.

"Heh. That country is less about machine technology and more about ship-building technology," said Hugo. "For example, steamships aren't uncommon among their people, but there are no automobiles to speak of. In a sense, Granvaloa is more unbalanced than Dryfe. After all, though their magic technology is behind that of most countries, their magic ships are unmatched."

"So that's how it is," I nodded. Though it was limited to shipbuilding, the maritime nation excelled in both magic and technology.

Yeah, it's safe to call it unbalanced, I thought.

"Also," added Hugo. "Since they're the only ones salvaging things from underwater ruins, not even Dryfe knows what they really have."

Well, that sure piqued my interest. I should go there someday.

"Hmm… Hugo," Nemesis spoke up. "Did you get the knowledge about this civilization from the world's official description?"

"No," he answered. "I've been told about it by archeologist tians and some trivia-crazed acquaintances who've explored ruins all over the world. The clan I belong to has many people with strange hobbies."

"Your clan?" I asked.

"Yes," Hugo nodded. "It's one of the bigger clans in Dryfe, so there are quite a lot of us. If you ever switch to serving the imperium, I'll help you join."

"Ha ha ha," I laughed. "I don't see that happening."

"Heh. I think that depends on the results of the upcoming war."

He wasn't wrong. That could easily happen if the imperium came out on top and the kingdom became its domain.

"Though it's not impossible that the results lead to me joining *your* clan," he added.

"My own clan, huh?" I said. "I actually don't have one yet."

"Then you should find one that has people you get along with and join it. It'll give you more things to do in this world. You can also make one yourself, if you like."

"I'll think about it... Oh?" I said, startled.

As we made our way through the forest, the Magingear had lowered its engine's output and reduced its noise to a minimum.

"Looks like we're here," said Hugo.

A few moments later, we came close to the forest's edge.

"I see it," Cyco said.

I looked through the spaces between the trees.

Outside the forest was a large building — a stone fortress. With its walls covered in ivy, it stood in the middle of a forest clearing that extended for at least a few hundred meters in every direction.

It was easy to tell that it had been built a long time ago, eventually been abandoned, and was now being used as the bandits' hideout.

"It's just like it was shown on the map," said Hugo. "That's the place, no doubt about it. There're even some guards there."

He was right — I could see some bandits standing on the fortress' walls. However, the boredom in their mannerisms and the occasional yawns made it obvious that they weren't too serious about their job. At the very least, they still hadn't noticed us hiding in the forest.

I had my worries about the possibility of them seeing Magingear, but that didn't seem to be necessary. The trees in the forest were tall enough to hide it without any problem. The dark green coating probably worked as a good camouflage, too.

"What now?" asked Nemesis. "Shall we all charge at it?"

"Don't be stupid," I said. "It'll all be over if they start using the kidnapped children as hostages."

Then again, that was going to happen in any scenario where we made an attempt to fight the bandits and do the rescuing. However, since we didn't know the inner structure of the fortress, sneaking in without getting spotted would be difficult. Also, no matter how negligent the guards were, they'd quickly notice us if we showed ourselves in this wide open space.

"...I happen to have an idea on how to go about this," said Hugo.

"An idea?" I asked.

The Magingear he was driving nodded in a highly convincing manner and pointed at itself.

"Everyone in this world knows that this weapon belongs to Dryfe," he said. That was the reason why we got here through a route on which no one could see us.

"Again, this is *a weapon belonging to Dryfe*," he continued. "The same Dryfe that has *absolutely no reason to save the kingdom's children*."

"Hm...? Ah!" I finally realized what he meant. "If I attack the fortress, they will likely think that it has nothing to do with the kidnappings. After all, there's no reason for a man of the imperium to come rescue the children of an enemy nation. That will prevent the bandits from using them as hostages. They will probably believe that I wouldn't discriminate and kill any children they brought out, and that would be unfavorable for them because less children means less ransom money."

So, Hugo's true affiliation is actually gonna be useful to us, huh? I thought.

"They won't be able to use the children as hostages," he continued. "And they certainly won't just sit and do nothing while I attack the fortress. They will surely come to face me. And while they're busy with me, you can sneak into the building and rescue the kidnapped children. That's the plan I have in mind, anyway."

"Sounds good," I nodded. "Are you sure you'll be okay, though? Being a distraction isn't easy."

"A Marshall II has a strong frame," said Hugo. "It won't go down easily. Also, I have Cyco with me."

"Yep," she nodded. "What do we do?"

"You use Enemy Detect," Hugo said. "Also, ready some Smoke Dischargers to make a smokescreen for us to hide in while we lower their numbers."

"Oui, umm… monsieur."

"You can use the smoke to close in on the fortress," Hugo added, turning to me. "Save the children, and stay out of sight."

"All right," I nodded.

"Understood!" Nemesis declared. "This is nothing Ray and I can't do!"

"It will probably be a battle against time," Hugo added. "You will need to be both fast and precise."

"I know," I nodded again. A battle against time while trying to save children. It was going to be much like my first quest, when I'd had to save Milianne.

However, back then, I'd had Liliana and — most of all — my brother with me. Without him, I couldn't have made my way to where Milianne was, and if he hadn't kept the Demi-Dragon Worms busy, the situation would've gotten much worse.

Also, that had been a difficulty level 5 quest. The quest we were doing right now was a difficulty level 8. I had no idea what kind of monsters I would have to face, and I didn't have the people I'd relied on back when I'd saved Milianne.

Still, this time, I had Hugo and Cyco with me. I was stronger, as well, and Nemesis was more reliable than ever. I didn't know how far that would get me, but...

"...Backing out isn't really an option when the lives of children are on the line."

"Hm?" Hugo asked.

Wait, did I say that out loud? I thought. Hugo had apparently heard what I'd said and stared at me with the Magingear's head camera.

"What?" I asked.

Well, I kinda understood what he wanted to say. He probably thought I was getting a bit too serious about *Infinite Dendrogram*, which — from beginning to the end — was nothing but a game. However, game or not, having children die on me left a bad taste in my mouth.

Hugo stayed silent. He looked at me through the camera while thinking about something.

"If you've got something to say, just say it," I said.

"...All right." Hugo finally spoke up. His words were far from what I'd expected. "It's nothing much... I just realized that you, too, are a real Maiden's Master."

"Hm?" I raised an eyebrow. I didn't see what he meant by that. I wasn't aware of any relationship between what I'd said and the fact that I was the Master of Nemesis, a Type Maiden.

"Do you know what Masters of Type Maiden Embryos have in common?" he asked.

"They have something in common?" I asked back.

"Yes. A Master I know told me that such Masters have a certain common feature."

I had yet to meet a single other Maiden's Master, but I was mildly surprised to hear that we all had a similarity. "Which is...?"

"They don't feel *Infinite Dendrogram* is a mere game."

...*What?*

"That's stupid," I said. "I'm well aware that we're in a game here."

I had no grand delusions about being in an old light novel type of scenario in which the game I'd started playing was actually a real other world. *Infinite Dendrogram* was a game, and I wouldn't argue against that.

"The Master I mentioned said the same thing," said Hugo. "However, somewhere deep inside, they don't believe that to be true. And that's why..." He fell silent.

"Why... what?" I asked.

"It's nothing. Never mind. Sorry for saying something weird right when we're about to attack the fortress. I got a bit derailed."

Damn it, don't leave me hanging after getting my attention like that! I thought.

"Oh, by the way," he spoke up again. "The enemies might be tians, but killing them doesn't count as a crime when they're criminals or if you're just defending yourself. Keep that in mind."

"Yeah... I will," I nodded.

After that, Hugo fell silent once again.

I'm still wondering what he was going to say, though, I thought.

"Master," Nemesis spoke to me telepathically.

What?

"Do you know what he was about to say?" she asked.

No, I don't. You don't either, right?

"I wouldn't say so. But if you say you don't know, it might be best for you if things stay that way."

"Hm?" I raised an eyebrow. *What do you mean by that?*

"Ray!" yelled Hugo in surprise. "Look over there!" Cutting short my conversation with Nemesis, his Magingear pointed at the fortress. I looked in that direction and saw that its gates were slowly opening.

"Look there," said Cyco. "A carriage is coming." I shifted my gaze to where she was pointing and saw a mountain road leading through an opening in the forest surrounding the fortress.

On it, there were several carriages moving towards the bandit hideout.

"Did they kidnap more children?" I asked.

"Seems like it," said Hugo.

"They're saying something," Cyco muttered. She placed her hands on her ears, closed her eyes, and focused her hearing. "'When we're back in the fortress'... 'we'll kill him'... 'our buddies'... 'got caught'... 'revenge'... 'we're killing'... 'the brat.'"

"Crap!" A realization made me mutter my frustration.

"Wait, do they mean...?!" Hugo seemed to have realized it, too.

They were talking about the five underlings we'd beaten, caught, and handed over to the guards.

"It seems there were more than those five," Hugo muttered. "They've noticed what we did back there."

And if that was the case, then the first child they were going to kill when they reached the fortress was the very same one we had to save.

"It seems like time is short." Hugo made the Magingear go from a kneeling position to standing upright. "I'll attack the ones at the carriages. That should make the ones in the fortress come out and help them. When that happens, I'll create a smokescreen you can use to get in undetected. Cyco, you support me."

"All right!" I nodded.

"Understood!" said Nemesis in her sword form.

"Yes, sir!" Cyco snapped to attention.

As soon as he confirmed that everyone was fine with his plan, Hugo made his Magingear jump out of the forest and charge at the bandits.

This time, he wasn't running like when we had traversed the forest. Instead, he used the wheels installed in its legs to do a rolling dash that made him the fastest I've seen yet. Not slowing down, he took out a gun that was mounted on the robot's pelvic area and began firing at the front of the group of carriages.

A single attack was enough to make the horses drawing the first carriage burst, while the resulting shockwave blew the coachman away and made the carriage fall to its side.

The sudden disaster made the carriages trailing behind it stop, and the Magingear — not letting the opportunity go to waste — began firing at and instantly killing the bandits surrounding them.

"Hm?" The sight actually made me feel strangely uncomfortable. Nemesis seemed to notice my reaction, but chose not to say anything.

After a number of bandits had been killed by Hugo's preemptive attacks, they finally began retaliating and fighting back. However, they weren't coordinated in any sense of the word, attacking independently with the methods each of them were familiar with.

Some used swords, fists, and axes, while others took the ranged approach with bows and arrows.

Reason stated that such things would be able to do nothing against the Magingear — which was as tough as a tank — but we were in *Infinite Dendrogram*. The bandits likely had low-rank battle-oriented jobs. Due to that, their stats would be higher than those of normal people, allowing their attacks to occasionally break and pierce through the Magingear's armor.

"Hghh!" Hugo exclaimed as his Marshall II showed no sign of stopping. He used the robot's army knife to cut down anyone who got too close.

Well, the term "knife" was only appropriate when compared to the Magingear. It was equivalent to a longsword for any bandit and it had absolutely no trouble slicing through their armor and splitting their torsos.

Hugo used the gun to shoot down anyone attacking him from a distance. The bullets were equivalent to cannon shots, and they made the bow-wielding bandits burst and scatter in all directions.

Though the bandits greatly outnumbered him, Hugo was far stronger than all of them combined. The sight made me recall the way Marilyn — Rook's Demi-Dragon — had gone rampaging within the army of Goblins. The robot was probably as powerful as she was. When he'd gotten in, Hugo had called it a "Demi-Dragon-Rank Magingear," and it was clear that the description was appropriate.

Hugo was also highly skilled at controlling it, and from what he'd told me on the way here, the Piloting skill he had from being in the Pilot job grouping greatly increased the stats of the machines he rode. As a result of all of that, he had an upper hand in this battle despite the bandits greatly outnumbering him.

"But his advantage isn't absolute," I muttered.

Though the bandits were dying one after the other, some of their attacks were landing on the Magingear. Little by little, the damage done by them was piling up and becoming obvious.

"Flaw," Cyco said from beside me. Then she told me about the robot's greatest disadvantage.

"Magingears can't be healed," she said. "They need to be stored and fixed."

"I see." I nodded.

Though fueled by magic, the Magingears were machines. Healing magic and medicine didn't work on them like they worked on people and monsters. Due to the constantly falling HP and the per-second MP cost, these iron giants could only fight for a limited amount of time.

And yet, for the sake of saving the children, Hugo played his part in the plan by facing the bandits head-on and distracting them.

"That's why we have to do our best, too," said Cyco.

"Of course," I agreed.

All at once, several dozens of bandits ran out of the fortress. They went to help their endangered comrades by joining their battle against the Magingear, but that came at the cost of reducing their numbers at the hideout.

"Now," Cyco said.

At about the same time…

…the Magingear covered the area in can-like objects it had kept around its waist. After rolling on the ground a bit, they began spinning around while intensely releasing great amounts of white smoke.

"Smoke Dischargers, released," said Cyco. "We can go now."

She disappeared from my side. Not only that, she disappeared from the party window, as well. Whether that mattered or not, she'd probably gone to assist Hugo.

"We're going too, Nemesis!" I said.

"Understood!" she agreed.

As the white smoke covered the surroundings, I tightened my grip on Nemesis in her sword form and ran towards the fortress.

I had to make good use of the opportunity Hugo had given me.

This was all to free the children and make sure they survived.

Letting the smoke shroud me, I broke into the fortress.

We'd saved Rebecca from her predicament in that back alley and instantly begun making our way to the hideout of the Gouz-Maise Gang for the sake of saving her little brother. That was why — by the time I broke into the fortress — I was grossly uninformed about what kind of group the Gouz-Maise Gang was. All I knew about them was that they were a bunch of scumbags who kidnapped and killed children.

I was far too clueless.

However, even if I'd known the kinds of things they actually did, it wouldn't have changed anything.

All that mattered was whether I was too late or not.

The smoke from the Smoke Dischargers used by Hugo's Magingear permeated even the interior of the fortress, allowing me to go through the entrance and reach the building's inner passages without being detected.

Despite the thick smoke overwhelming the rooms and hallways here, I didn't have any problem seeing which way was which. In fact, I could see right through it by merely straining my eyes a bit. I could only assume that it was made to not affect the vision of the user's — Hugo's — party members. I had no idea how that worked, though.

"Well, we're inside," said Nemesis. "But we don't know the structure of this place."

Since we had to be sneaky while moving through these hallways, Nemesis and I were talking to each other telepathically.

Every now and then, we passed by some bandits running to fight Hugo, but it was clear that they couldn't see us due to the smoke.

"Master, where do you think we can find the children?" she asked.

Either windowless rooms on the second floor or higher, or somewhere below.

"Why do you think that?"

The chances of them escaping would be higher if they were kept in the first floor, and I saw ivy growing on the walls around the windows of the upper floors. They could use that to go down and get out. By simple process of elimination, it's safe to guess that they're either below or above.

"Then they're probably underground," she said. "It's standard for kidnapping scoundrels to keep children locked up in the dungeon."

I didn't know if I could be as sure as her. However, the possibility was there, so I had no reason not to test it.

As those thoughts ran through my head, I came across a split in the hallway. There were three ways to go — forward, left, and right. A short distance up the right path, I saw a flight of stairs leading down — basically beckoning us in.

I chose to follow the call and went down underground.

"Ugh!" The moment I put my foot on the first stair, a strange stench came from the bottom and attacked my nose. It was a vile, yet familiar smell that I couldn't remember — or perhaps didn't want to. However, I couldn't back away just because of it, so I gathered my resolve and went further down.

The stairs, floor, walls, and ceiling were all made from stone, exactly as you'd expect. The ceiling was two times higher than my full height, while the distance between the walls was even greater than that.

I won't have any problems swinging Nemesis in here, I thought.

I also couldn't help but notice the unique humidity permeating the air and the dark green moss growing on the ceiling and the walls.

"How gloomy," commented Nemesis.

It's a dungeon, after all, I told her. *Also, this moss and humidity is a clear sign that there's underground water leaking in from somewhere.*

"Well, it's an abandoned fortress, after all."

Staying here for prolonged periods of time can't be good for the children's health.

"If the scoundrels cared about the little ones' health, they wouldn't be kidnapping or killing them."

...True that.

A single look at the underlings we'd beaten in the back alley or the ones around the carriages was enough to know that they didn't care for the children's lives whatsoever. Just remembering their words and behavior made me sick.

"Gh..."

"Do you feel it, Master?" asked Nemesis. She didn't say what she meant by "it." However, I knew without her having to put it into words.

"It started when I began going down the stairs," I said with my mouth. I finally recalled where I last breathed this stench.

There was no need to speak telepathically anymore. Hiding was unnecessary...

...because something at the other end of the hallway had already noticed us.

"There's something there..." said Nemesis.

"Yeah," I nodded.

I was being assaulted by multiple smells. The smell of the wafting humidity, the stuffy air, and the moss covering the walls mixed with the stench of blood and rotten meat. I was familiar with this smell because it had been all around me during my night in the Tomb Labyrinth. There was no way I could mistake it.

"Uuuaaaagghhh..." A groan reached my ears. It was followed by the rattling of bones. The sounds completed the imagery and made me all the more certain that the smell was that of the "undead."

Wounded Zombies were groaning as they closed in on me. Their decaying flesh clung to their bones, vile juices leaking from pustules and boils. The Civilian Skeletons closed the distance between us, their teeth rattling as they shambled ahead.

The sight robbed me of words. That reaction might've been unwarranted, given that I had already faced undead monsters in the Tomb Labyrinth, but there was an important difference between the Zombies and Skeletons there and the ones before me.

It wasn't the number of them. Sure, there were several dozens of them, but the difference I had in mind was far more important.

It wasn't their physical might, either. A single look was enough to tell that these undead were significantly weaker than the ones in the Tomb Labyrinth.

The great difference I had in mind was that they were all *the result of someone's death.*

"…F-Fuck off."

I didn't know who I was talking to — probably the vile reality that had allowed the sight to happen — but those words were the first to escape my lips before I began repeating them in my head.

"How horrid…" Nemesis broke in.

I closed my mouth, rage overcoming me in the form of a dull grind of tooth against tooth, while Nemesis — despite having a phobia of the dead — showed far more pity than fear.

The undead horde was composed of very small skeletons. I was about two times taller than any of them.

They were numerous enough to cover the whole hallway.

Nobody had to say it. I knew exactly who they had been before they were… this.

"I'm gonna be sick…"

The tiny undead closed in on us, extending their little arms. Grasping worn-out weapons, they slowly charged at us — the intruders.

I'd seen similar things in the Tomb Labyrinth, but undead that were made from the corpses of people were far too different from those that were created as undead to begin with. Just looking at them was enough to fill me with emotions that I could hardly bear.

"It appears that the bandits have someone who can use necromancy among them," said Nemesis. "They've repurposed the children they killed."

"Are you okay, Nemesis?" I asked.

"Ha!" she laughed with no humor in her tone. "My fear is irrelevant right now. How could they do this to children?"

"I feel the same," I said.

With my eyes fixed on the undead horde, I couldn't help but wonder whether it was possible to save them. But I already knew the answer to that. The children were lost.

If there was a way to bring people back from the dead, this war-ravaged country would've done it ages ago. That meant that it either didn't exist or it was a method that even the kingdom couldn't do. As things were, I simply couldn't save them.

"Tell me, Nemesis," I spoke up.

"What is it?" she asked.

"What happens to the undead when they die?"

The undead in the Tomb Labyrinth — a created dungeon — weren't actual corpses, but mere creations. However, though they had the same names as the monsters back there, these Wounded Zombies and Civilian Skeletons before me had once been living beings. That made me wonder about what would become of their souls.

"I do not know," said Nemesis with a regretful tone. "Some are being used as nothing but empty corpses, while others still have their souls trapped in the bodies. I am not one to know what would happen to them when the vessels are destroyed."

"I see..."

"However, I believe it's best to end their painful existence as undead," she added.

"...Yeah."

The distance between me and the undead children became a mere five meters.

The dimly-shining lights on the walls lit up the faces of the zombies and made me painfully aware that some of them had traces of facial features from when they had been alive.

I tightly closed my eyes and stayed like that for a few seconds. Then I opened them and directed the back of my left hand at the undead children.

"I'm sorry."

I made my left Miasmaflame Bracer burn them all with a stream of Purgatorial Flames. Their thin bones, decaying flesh, and what little hair they had left were embraced by the intense blaze and quickly burned away. It only took a moment for them to lose their HP and continue burning as actual corpses, rather than undead monstrosities.

A black smoke shrouded the hallway before beginning to follow the ceiling up the stairs and mix with the white smokescreen.

I ended the flow of fire, making them stop burning, and leave behind nothing but cremated remains.

[Successfully eliminated over 100 monsters that fit the condition "Undead of the appropriate total level"]
[Due to fulfilling the job condition, "Paladin" and the elimination total condition, "Eliminate 100 appropriate monsters," the skill "Purifying Silverlight" has been acquired]

A message told me that I'd learned a new skill, but I felt no joy from the news. My heart was bogged down.

I stood silently. I slowly put my hands together. Like I would do while standing before a grave, I prayed for their happiness in the next world.

All of a sudden, an airflow created by the heat made a gust of wind pass through this underground hallway.

"*T h a n k y o u.*"

As the wind blew by, those words entered my ears.

But I was certain it was just wishful thinking on my part. It was an illusion born out of my wish that their souls were saved.

"Master," Nemesis called out to me.

"Is this it, Nemesis?" I asked while placing my hand on my chest and trying to bear the heaviness of the situation. "Is this... Is this the feeling Hugo was going to mention back then?"

"...Yes," she said. "If, somewhere deep inside, Maiden's Masters don't believe this world to be just a game... If you acknowledge this world's lives to be just as real as those of your world..."

I was silent.

"...then the weight of the lives you shoulder in *Infinite Dendrogram* is much too real for you."

"Too real, huh?" I asked. The harsh reality of the heaviness of life. "You're probably right..."

This world was so realistic that it was hard to tell it apart from reality. Somewhere deep inside, I even believed that the tians living here actually had minds and souls. Even if my head told me that it was all just a game, I wasn't able to shake that feeling. That was why seeing tians die to Gardranda had left such a bad taste in my mouth. It was also the reason why I'd gone all out to protect Milianne from such an ending.

This case was no different. Except now, all I had before me were a bunch of people who had reached such sad conclusions.

I didn't know the courses of their lives. I had no idea how they'd ended up like this. They had been nowhere near me, so there was no way for me to know. However, the way they'd ended was just far too cruel for me to disregard it as your everyday tragedy, and the feelings overwhelming my heart were too powerful to ignore.

An aftertaste so bad that it seemed to burn my throat now permeated my chest, mixing with great amounts of sadness and anger.

"In this world — where lives are lost far more easily than in yours — this disposition you have might bring you great pain," said Nemesis.

"...That's true," I said weakly. I was actually on the verge of crying. It was so bad that a part of me wanted to throw it all away.

I probably wasn't the first to feel this way. Many of those who shared my nature probably couldn't stand to experience this overwhelming pain of loss more than once and instead chose to never touch *Infinite Dendrogram* again. A side of me was actually urging me to do the same.

"However, I... Not yet." I was still unbroken.

I still had to save the rest of the children. I still had a promise to fulfill.

And most of all, I still had to make sure that the shithead who'd created this sight got what was coming to him. I had to make him pay.

I shifted my gaze to the children — now nothing but dust.

Hidden under their remains was a piece of metal that had something written on it in *Infinite Dendrogram*'s common language.

It said "Maise's Utility Child Civilian Skeleton, Specimen No. 87."

It was a tag. That was all that child had been to the one who'd put it on.

The words and the number on it made me all the more aware that this enemy of mine was beyond redemption. Whether this was a game or not, I simply couldn't let him be.

"Let's go, Nemesis," I said. "We're bound to find him at the end of this hallway."

"Understood!"

And so, we began walking forward.

One of the two leaders of the Gouz-Maise Gang — Lich Maise.

"Hm?" I said. A drop in my Minion Capacity count made me aware that some of the undead under my command had vanished.

To be more specific, the dead units had just been the trash I'd made to kill some time. I'd left those little things in the underground hallway to act as sentries.

They were weak, so their only use had been as alarms. I had gotten worried about nothing. I'd thought I might've lost something of actual value.

It did catch me by surprise, however. I'd been aware that some intruder was causing a ruckus on the surface, but I'd had no idea that there was someone underground, as well.

"Gouz." I used a magic item that kept me in contact with the surface.

"Yeah?" he asked.

"How are things up there?" I asked.

"I give it five or six more minutes," Gouz answered. "It should all be over by then."

"In that case, when our underlings are all dead, move in to crush the intruder," I said. "I'll take care of the rat here in the dungeon. Once it's dealt with, we're moving."

"Gotcha," he said. "Oh yeah, it looks like this'll get me lots of packed lunches, so take some extra inventories for me, will ya?"

"Of course." I had some empty inventories meant for corpse retrieval somewhere around here. I intended to take everything with me along with the inventory containing my ultimate treasure and ritual.

"Once you're done with the intruder, wait in front of the gate," I said.

"Sure," Gouz said.

I cut the connection.

That's the surface taken care of, I thought. Though our underlings were all weaklings still sitting on their first low-rank jobs, having faced all of them and surviving was no simple task. It meant that the intruder was quite tough. However, Gouz was on another level.

He'd reached the maximum level, had a high-rank job, and — when it came to the entire gladiator job grouping — he was surely among the top five in this country. If Figaro hadn't existed, it wouldn't have been strange for Gouz to have taken the seat of the Over Gladiator.

I, too, was at the maximum level. Not only that, but I was at this country's pinnacle when it came to necromancy, and had a Superior Job within arms' reach. I didn't know how powerful the intruders were, but as long as they weren't Superiors and didn't have Superior Jobs, there was nothing for us to fear.

However, something about them was highly curious.

"Just what *is* their business here?" I muttered. They should've been well aware by now that trying to eliminate us was not worth the effort.

Are they interested in our treasure? I thought. Even when the amount I sent to Caldina was considered, the money we had with us was great. If someone wanted to get rich quick, taking it would be a perfectly viable method.

However, if they were actually planning to delve into such daredevilry, it told me everything I needed to know about them.

"Well, now... I believe it is time to prepare a welcome to my inhuman intruder."

Chapter Four ⟩ The Two Leaders

High Pilot Hugo Lesseps

The clan I was part of was a gathering of players that mostly focused on crafting.

Engineers, Mechanics, Pharmacists, Smiths... This world had many such jobs that produced all sorts of things, but when the work of tians and players was compared, most of the time, players were the ones that came out on top.

Just like with battle jobs, this was due to the abilities and bonuses to stat growth given to them by their Embryos. The quality of the item and the production success rate were dependent on skill level and DEX — not any real-life ability. Due to that, even a player who was a novice at the craft could produce work showing true mastery.

As my clan leader often said: "Unlike battle — which now involves moving your body — production in this game isn't too different from how it was when MMORPGs weren't VR. That's why even the slowest klutz can do it."

That wasn't all, though.

"Mind you, that only applies when they're making something that has already been made," he liked to continue. "To create something new, you need the power to imagine it. When making something without the instructions, the necessary materials and inventiveness are on a completely different level."

Infinite Dendrogram's crafting came in two types — the production of known items and the creation of new items.

Both methods required the person to have sufficient materials, skills, and stats.

However, while known items could easily be made by following the instructions displayed on Recipes, the creation of new items required the creation of those very instructions.

Naturally, they weren't easy to make, since they required a deeper understanding of the processes involved, detailed knowledge of this world's science and magic, and a proper grasp of the necessary materials.

Simply put, creating new items was far too taxing. Thus, even after half a year had passed since the game's release, Masters had still been making only known or slightly customized items.

That had changed with our clan.

Our clan leader had made a breakthrough in the game's crafting department. In hindsight, it had been pretty simple, for he'd merely begun gathering people who were skilled and knowledgeable in reality.

The Dryfe Imperium was a country that had machine technology. Though there were many differences — such as the fuel of the machines being magic — the Imperium's technology had similarities to what we had in reality. The clan leader had made good use of that fact.

He'd gathered various people who had knowledge about machines, which included graduate school students that had majored in mechanical engineering, skilled workers from automobile factories, designers of heavy machinery, and even those who were simply nutty about cars, trains, or weapons. And it was all for the goal of creating a new item.

Of course, people hadn't gone to him just because he was recruiting. The clan leader had begun to receive a significant amount of applications when he'd revealed a specific project of his.

Its goal was to create a humanoid battle robot.

Back then, Dryfe hadn't had any humanoid mobile weapon-type Magingears. When the game had begun, the only Magingears Dryfe had had in their arsenal were the powered suits nicknamed "Marshall" and the tanks known as "Geist." While bipedal, human-like robots weren't even being invented. Thus, the clan leader had made it his goal to create them.

Many people had been intrigued by the idea, so by the time the clan had been created, it'd already had dozens of knowledgeable and skilled people. They'd all quickly begun cooperating and working towards the common goal.

"All you need is knowledge, equipment, manpower, materials, money, imagination, skill level, luck, and guinea pigs!" the leader had announced when he'd kickstarted the project.

Clearly, it had been a demanding task. However, they'd been able to prepare everything they needed.

They'd mixed and matched their knowledges of machinery, compared and adjusted their magic technology, and performed lots of trial and error while trying to make it all click. There had been countless failures, great costs, and members leaving one after the other. However, they'd continued despite the many problems.

One of the senior members had compared the whole thing to something called "Project X," and there had been many who'd nodded to his words. I had been uninformed and knew nothing about that show, but it seemed to click with those from his generation — especially the Japanese people.

And so, after two months in real life — half a year in *Infinite Dendrogram* — all the trouble has finally paid off as they completed a new item.

The name given to it was "Marshall II." It was a mass-producible weapon with the power equivalent of a Demi-Dragon. The humanoid battle robot Magingear was a straight upgrade to a Marshall — the powered suit.

Once the Marshall II was complete and the Recipe became public, our clan quickly began growing into the largest one in Dryfe Imperium.

The battle before the fortress was nearing its end.

"Hugo, five o'clock, one Gunner," said Cyco.

"Oui."

As Cyco scouted the fog and gave me directions, I acted accordingly by turning my frame and firing from the Hand Canon on my left hand.

The Gunner that was aiming at me with a magic gun failed to evade my attack, and the explosive shot from my MRW03 Hand Canon made him burst into little pieces, leaving only the arm that was gripping the weapon.

That gun is one of the Imperium's older models, I thought. *Looks like our technology is leaking through that country's black market again.*

"Six o'clock, two Fighters," said Cyco.

"Got it."

I made my upper half turn around and used the centrifugal force to cut them down with my SRW02 Battle Knife.

The first one was unable to react as it broke through his armor, flesh, bone, flesh, armor — in that order — and split him at his torso. The second one reacted and stopped my Battle Knife with his greatshield.

Unlike in reality, *Infinite Dendrogram's* Fighters of this vein were tough. Though a Marshall II had power that made most heavy machinery pale in comparison, many Fighters could — evidently — block mine's attacks and even harm it.

This one had both reaction speed and power.

However...

"Your legs are wide open," I said.

Making sure he didn't move by forcing him to struggle against the force of my Battle Knife, I used the Marshall II's legs to step on his. The robot's overall weight — which reached a whole ten tons — was far too great for his plated boots to handle, and his legs were crushed.

"HHHH?!"

The moment he released a voiceless scream and lowered the power on his shield arm, I used my blade — now free to move — to split his head in half.

"No enemies nearby," said Cyco.

"Got it," I replied. "Continue keeping an eye out. And dedicate extra attention to the direction of the fortress."

"Oui."

Apparently, I'd handled everything they've sent at me so far. The realization that I'd prevailed made me heave a deep sigh.

My Marshall II was standing in the middle of the battlefield, surrounded by countless bandit corpses. I silently looked around. The one responsible for this horrible scene was me.

I was fully aware that there were things to be said about me killing so many people, but my actions didn't make my heart hurt, nor did I regret them.

I'd known about the existence of the Gouz-Maise Gang before Rebecca had told me about them. In fact, I'd been aware of them before I'd even come to Gideon. During the research we'd done for *the plan*, I'd noticed them among the factions surrounding the city and engraved them onto my mind.

They had killed far too many children and far too many noble souls trying to save them. It was only natural for people who took the lives of other humans to — in turn — be killed by them, as well. I thoroughly believed that to be true.

Though, considering that I was an immortal Master, that belief might be insolent and contradictory.

"All right, now…" I muttered.

Though the result of the battle made it seem like my victory had been flawless, that was far from the truth. My own HP hadn't dropped a single percent, but the damage to my Marshall II was severe. Due to the attacks it had sustained, about a third of its armor had come off, which had exposed the inner frame to considerable amounts of damage. The movement of its left arm had become quite slow, as well.

Special equipment like cars, ships, and Magingear didn't have any HP displays, but if they did, my Marshall II's gauge would be at about 30% of the total. That was a testament to just how difficult the battle had been.

Though a Marshall II was a humanoid robot straight out of science fiction, my opponents were all true inhabitants of this fantasy world. The axes they'd swung could break steel, and the arrows they'd fired had easily pierced through the robot's armor. If my fellow clan members hadn't increased the Marshall II's stats by fine tuning it for better use by the clan's Masters, and if I hadn't given it the bonuses from a High Pilot riding it, I would've been overwhelmed by their numbers and lost.

I sighed yet again, reached into my inventory and took out an MP Recovery Potion.

Moving and fighting in the Magingear came at a cost to my MP. During the battle, it had dropped to a mere 20% of the total, and if I didn't restore it, the damage to my Marshall II would be the least of my worries in the upcoming battles.

"Hugo," Cyco addressed me.

I drank the contents of the bottle and replied to her. "What is it, Cyco?" "It wouldn't have been this hard if you'd used your Embryo's skill," she said.

"Indeed." I nodded in response. She was completely right. If I'd used my Embryo's skill, I could've won without getting as much as a scratch on me. After all, it was basically the natural enemy of people such as these.

However…

"I can't," I said. "I will only allow myself to use that skill after the plan begins. I am not touching it before that. That's an order from the clan leader, and I made a promise to follow it."

"But no one's watching — not even Ray."

"Even so," I said. "If I were to use the skill before the plan begins, it would have to be a situation when I simply *have* to do it." And thankfully, it hadn't come to that.

"How stubborn," she said.

"I'm aware," I nodded. "Now, I wonder if there are any kidnapped children in those carriages."

I could easily help them right now, but doing so would made it obvious that using them as hostages would be effective against me. If another battle began while they were aware of that, the scum would begin using them to threaten me.

That would be fine if there were no more bandits left or if Ray had exterminated all the ones still at the fortress, but if some were still alive, trying to help the children in the carriages would be dangerous. I had to leave them there for now.

As such thoughts went through my head...

"...Heh," I grinned.

"Hugo," said Cyco.

"I know."

I sighed slightly and moved the levers to make the Magingear replace the Hand Cannon's empty explosive shot magazine with a full one it had hanging on its waist. Even while doing such a simple action, I couldn't help but be aware that the left arm's movements were noticeably duller.

"I could've put the Marshall II back in the Garage and fixed it up, but it seems I'll have to give up on that," I said. After all — I was all out of time.

Aiming towards the entrance of the fortress, I fired a shot from my Hand Cannon. It went through the open gates and exploded upon hitting the *thing* standing right behind them.

Any normal human hit by such an attack would've burst into pieces so small that none of them would've reached one kilogram in mass. However, that didn't happen to the creature standing there.

"Damn, that hurts!" it said. "It's kinda hot, too."

With those words, the thing showed itself while displaying no signs of injury or pain.

It was a demon of a large stature. Despite its head being that of an ox, the teeth lining its mouth were all hound-like fangs.

Its height almost matched that of my Marshall II. It even had to bend a bit to fit through the fortress' gates, which were twice as tall as the average person. A single glance was enough to know that it was on an entirely different level from the bandits I'd been fighting until now.

The sight of it made me tremble.

"...I assume you're one of the leaders of the Gouz-Maise Gang?" I asked.

"Ayup," it said. "Yer talkin' to one of the two great leaders of the Gouz-Maise Gang — Strong Gladiator Gouz."

"Hugo, do you know about category-based personality analysis?" the clan leader had asked soon after I'd joined the clan. It had happened about a month ago in terms of reality's time.

The clan had already become the largest in Dryfe. It was known for having played a great role in the war and was flourishing in terms of both budget and human resources. There was no end to the Masters trying to join, and the total number of members was quickly closing in on a thousand.

Back then, I had still been a rookie whose total *Infinite Dendrogram* playtime didn't even break a month — a Master who'd just happened to join at that particular time. However, due to some things in reality, the leader had taken an interest in me and invited me into his clan. Because of those circumstances, he and I often had talks such as these.

"Is it something like blood type-based personality analysis?" I asked. "It certainly sounds like it."

I wasn't fond of the idea behind blood type-based personality analysis. Rather than trying to research my character by examining the traits I was born with, I preferred to strive to be someone I wanted to be. A person's character was best left for the person to decide. Whether here or in reality, I sincerely believed that to be true.

"Blood types, eh?" said the leader. "I don't like personality analysis based on that because the basis for it is extremely weak. I still think that brain — not blood — should be the first thing to look at if you wanted to know how a person ticks. Well, anyway…"

He reached into his inventory and took out a whiteboard. Then he began writing something down on it with a marker. He liked explaining things, so he always had those objects with him.

He also liked scheming, so he often used them to lay out the plans that came to his mind. It wouldn't have been too bad if the schemes could be laughed off, but he often made plots which — while amusing to us — were nothing short of tragic to those affected.

A part of me was often disturbed by such plans, but the part of me that would stop him simply didn't exist.

…Back to the matter at hand.

On the whiteboard, the leader drew a humanoid shape which represented a Master and wrote down several Embryo categories to the side of it.

"You know how, in the Zeroth Form, an Embryo examines the Master's actions, character, and other personal things before using the results to go into the First Form, right? Well, some decided to turn it around, creating this idea that you can find out what kind of person a Master is by looking at the type of their Embryo."

That made sense. Since Embryos were born from the inner workings of Masters, they were far more reliable than blood types.

"The idea was popular about one year ago in terms of real time," said the leader. "I tried my hand at it, too. However, High-Rank Embryos and above had so many irregularities that I couldn't make sense of them at all. There were even some Embryos like mine — completely unique in terms of typing. In the end, the only results that were somewhat reliable were those I got from four of the five base categories and a certain extra."

The categories he wrote down were Arms, Guardian, Castle, Territory, and just "extra."

"Boss," I spoke up. "I don't see Chariot among the five main categories."

"Chariot, eh?" he repeated. "I actually didn't notice anything definite among Masters with those Embryos. That's why it's not in my results."

What a shame, I thought. I was actually quite curious about that category.

"Now, let me describe them for you," he said. "Arms often belong to people who are courageous and unafraid to get hurt. Reckless, stupid, emotional, hot-blooded. There are many ways to describe them. Guardian Masters are the opposite — they're cowardly, afraid to get hurt, lonely, or just want to have someone protect them. These two fit the general image, don't you think?"

Weapons and defenses. When the nature of those Embryos was considered, that evaluation seemed to be quite correct. Though I couldn't help but wonder where non-weapon Arms were in all of this.

"Castle Masters are introverted, gentle, careful, cooperative, and have an artisan's temperament. Seems right, no?" he said. "Territory Masters have a lust for control, tend to hoard their stress, create rules for themselves, and are self-righteous and lone wolves. By the way, my Embryo's first category was Castle."

I see, I thought. So, depending on the person, there was room for objections. Especially when you considered the leader's personality and aligned it with the description of Castle Masters.

"There are some hybrids that mix several categories at once, so it's hard to be completely sure," he added. "But anyway, that's the main categories covered."

"So, boss," I spoke up. "What's the extra category?"

"Maiden."

His answer made my eyes widen, though only a little bit.

"Type Maiden," he said. "A rare category you will encounter every now and then. These Embryos have two main features. First, they're always hybrids that come equipped with another category. And second, their base form is always that of a human. Sure, there are Guardians that take the shape of humanoid monsters, but Maidens are always humans, through and through."

I was fully aware of those features.

"Just so you know, the term 'Maiden' is only used when their human form is female," he continued. "It's different when it's male, but those are just so damn rare."

"So, leader… what are Maiden Masters like?" I asked.

"They don't think that this world is a game. To them, the weight of the lives here is just as great as it is in reality."

His answer made me silently gasp.

"So, got anything to say about my deductions, Hugo?"

I had trouble formulating an answer to that.

Finally, one of the two leaders of the gang had left the fortress and introduced himself as Gouz, the Strong Gladiator.

"Strong Gladiator" was one of the high-rank jobs from the gladiator grouping. I'd heard that it focused mainly on hand-to-hand combat. What mattered more than the job itself, however, was the fact that he even *had* a job, which meant that — despite appearing so monstrous — he was actually a Demi-Human. That reality was also supported by the fact that he could hold a conversation.

"Man, did you make a mess here," he said. "My boys were such a nice little bunch, and you went and killed them all."

"You say that," I replied, "but I don't see a hint of anger or sadness in you."

"Well, yeah, means I get a buncha free meals, right?"

…*This wretch,* I thought.

"A kid's meat is sweet and tender, sure," he continued. "But every now and then, I feel like sinking my teeth into the bitter meat of an adult. Did ya know that adult flesh actually becomes more bitter and tastier the more of a dreg they are?"

"Sorry, but I'm a vegetarian," I snapped.

"Really, now? Surprised ya can stay healthy like that. Guess that immortality you Masters have comes packaged with some tough bodies, eh?"

So he knew I was a Master.

"I was watchin' the whole fight from the fortress," he went on. "Your movements are too good. Don't hafta be a genius to see that you're not the usual soldier."

"Heh," I grinned. "Then you could've come out before I'd killed every single one of your underlings."

"Oh, but having you take care of them saved us the hassle," he said.

"...What?"

"Well, we were actually planning to move out of here," he explained. "By 'we,' I mean me and the other leader, of course. The underlings and the brats were just in the way, ya know? We planned to kill and eat them all."

The leaders were leaving their hideout and getting rid of their underlings? I thought. *What drove them to do that?*

"So what's the reason?" I asked.

"Not telling," he said. "Well, I don't actually need any reasons. He said we're doing it, so I'm just tagging along."

So the other leader was above him, while he merely acted as his right hand man.

...That relationship reminded me of a certain someone.

"Thanks to you killing our underlings, all that's left is to eat 'em," he added. "Then just gotta take care of the brats in the dungeon... and the ones the boys just brought us."

He shifted his gaze towards the carriages behind me... specifically, towards the children inside.

"I won't allow that," I said coldly. I made my Marshall II brandish the Battle Knife and aim the Hand Cannon at him.

"Ha ha ha!" he laughed. "Thought as much. But..."

Gouz lowered his center of gravity, and...

"Y'CAN'T WIN AGAINST ME WITH THAT BROKEN PILE OF JUNK, YA DUMB SHIT!"

...with a roar that seemed to shake the fortress — no, the whole ground around him — he charged at me while perking his shoulders.

In response to that unrefined — almost suicidal — attack, I swung my Battle Knife at him. Since the explosive shot from my Hand Cannon hadn't worked, I chose to use my melee weapon — a means of attack with a more focused type of damage — to hit his weak point. Specifically, I aimed at his carotid artery, which was sure to become a fatal injury when damaged.

However, the result was far from my expectations.

"NOT GONNA WORK!"

My Battle Knife actually broke — not by his horns or claws, but by the skin covering his carotid artery.

"Huh?!" I exclaimed.

A moment later, Gouz's large body rammed into my Marshall II and greatly shook the inside of the cockpit.

"MGHHHOOOOOO!"

Though the robot was several times heavier than him, his power was great enough to overcome that difference in weight. After

143

pushing the Marshall II for more than ten meters, Gouz grabbed hold of its torso and threw it in an uncertain direction. Following a momentary floating sensation, the Marshall II crashed into the ground.

"Ghh! Ahhh!" Though the harness fixing me to the machine didn't show any signs of letting go, the force of the impact made the air escape my lungs. I hurriedly tried to regain my breath, but my respiratory system didn't seem to be functioning properly.

I then tried to move the levers to make the Magingear get into a proper position, but it didn't go too well. The Marshall II or myself — I couldn't tell which one was broken.

"Hugo!" said Cyco.

"Heh… ha ha ha," I laughed. "I underestimated him. This ox-head's tough. Clearly among the best high-rank job wielders. He could even aim for a Superior Job if the conditions were right."

However, that couldn't ever happen because the Superior Job of the gladiator grouping — Over Gladiator — had already been taken by that "Figaro" fellow.

Still, there was no denying that Gouz was strong. He could easily defeat high-rank Masters such as myself. Honestly, I wasn't certain if I could've won against him even if the Marshall II had been in perfect shape.

This robot's ability was equivalent to that of a Demi-Dragon. My level 7 Piloting skill increased its power by 140%, but that still wasn't enough to match this man.

"Hugo," Cyco said again.

"Yes, I can hear you, Cyco," I responded.

"Will you use the skill?" she asked.

I was silent. I still didn't know if that was a good idea.

My power was below that of Gouz. The gap between us was made even greater by the damage I'd sustained.

The Marshall II and I can't hope to win against this tough man-eater, I thought. *However, if I use the skill — my Embryo's skill — the result will change drastically. My victory will become certain due to the fact that he is a tough man-eater.*

However, I'd made it a point not to use my Embryo's skill until the project, and...

"Man, I'm really workin' up an appetite here," he cut my thoughts short with his words.

Hearing Gouz say that, I looked at him through the Marshall II's cracked camera-eye. Despite being in battle with me, he was facing towards the other direction. Considering my condition, he might've been thinking that the battle was over.

Gouz was messing with a corpse of one of his underlings. He removed the armor, stripped off the clothes... and sank his fangs into the flesh.

"Mm, them's good eatin'," he spoke while eating, courtesy be damned. "It's just so... complete. Wouldn't expect less from my boys."

With those words, bite by bite, he devoured his underling whole. As the sight filled me with an urge to vomit, I looked at my equipment window and tested the levers to determine the Marshall II's condition.

More than 70% of the armor was lost, while the damage to the armor that remained was critical. The left arm wasn't moving at all. The right arm's movements were dull. The legs, however, were still mobile.

As for weapons... the Hand Cannon had been lost along with the left hand. The Battle Knife had been completely destroyed. The Marshall II had been rendered useless for battle.

"My choices are..."

...to use the skill or retreat without using it, I thought.

I couldn't use the skill because of the plan.

I couldn't let myself get the death penalty here because the plan was commencing tomorrow.

Thus, I had to run away...

But if I retreated, Ray was still here. There was the possibility that he could defeat Gouz. Therefore, even if I retreated...

"Main course over — guess I'll have dessert!" He cut my thoughts short again and took something out of the bag hanging at his waist.

Once I realized what it was... my mind almost blanked out completely.

The thing in Gouz's hand was about the size of a ball. Small eyes — open wide and filled with terror, swaying hair — long and drenched in blood... It was unmistakably a human head. The head of a little girl.

Gouz threw it into his mouth as nonchalantly as one would a piece of candy. The demonic fangs lining his oral cavity fell downwards, mashing the child's skull with ease.

"Man, it's so good," he said. "Kid meat's tastiest when they know they're about to die, y'know that? But my appetite ain't quite sated yet."

Saying that, Gouz began making his way towards the carriage, and his intentions became immediately clear.

"Gh…" The deed I'd just witnessed and the realization of what he was going to do made all the hesitation in my mind fade away like it had never been there. What took its place was pure, unadulterated wrath.

"Hugo!" Cyco called out to me again.

"Cyco," I replied.

"Will you use the skill?"

"*You* already know the answer to that."

Though it was still severely damaged, I made my Marshall II stand upright.

"Gouz!" I yelled.

The ox-head turned around when he heard his own name called out.

"Huhh? Ya still awake, ya Master piece of shit?" he asked.

Awake? I repeated the word in my head. *How appropriate.*

Indeed — I had been half-asleep until now. I hadn't used the skill because of the plan. And because of the same plan, I'd chosen to avoid getting the death penalty and run away.

How thoroughly absurd. That wasn't *me* at all.

The Hugo Lesseps I strived to be wasn't this unsightly an individual.

Thus, I made my wrath known.

"I declare that I will no longer tolerate you!"

My words made Gouz laugh. "Ha ha ha! Big words, comin' from a Master who treats my entire world like a little game! You aren't the first of your kind to come here, and let me tell ya — none of the ones before ya were actually serious about whatever they were doing. You shits can't die in this world, so what's it matter to you? You can't ever know the fear of death my kind know!"

"Indeed," I said. "We Masters all enter this world with the intention to play. However, there are some that listen to the voices of those who call this world their home. Some that grieve when hearing the dying cries of the weak. And some who use that to set what they really are."

Thus, I had decided on my role in this world.

I was the thorn of a rose. A spike meant to pierce any and all scoundrels trying to ravage beautiful flowers and precious lives.

That was the true Hugo Lesseps. The role I'd willingly given to myself.

"Be aware," I said. "For the sin of ending lives too many to count, I will send you into the bowels of Hell."

Following the set role, I faced the scoundrel — Gouz — and declared, "My hell will destroy you." He would pay for all his sins.

"DO YOUR WORST, YA PIECE OF SHIT!" Gouz screamed in exasperation, and charged at me once again.

Another attack from him could completely destroy the Marshall II and kill me alongside it. However, that had no chance of happening at this point.

"Cyco!"

Cyco stood up on the robot's shoulder.

"Crest Disguise... Disable," she said. Through the camera-eye, I could see Gouz's face fill with surprise. It was only natural, considering what he'd just seen.

Cyco suddenly appeared on the Marshall II and made the crest on her left hand — the proof of a Master — disappear.

Indeed — Cyco was not a Master.

A Master of that name simply didn't exist.

Cyco's true identity was...

"Cocytus, it's time."

"Yes, Master."

Cyco — Cocytus — disintegrated to become a gathering of white and blue particles that showered the Marshall II, merged with it, and drastically changed its appearance.

The surroundings were momentarily overwhelmed by a whirling blizzard, followed by a brief whiteout.

In the center of it all stood Cocytus and I — taking the shape of a completely reconstructed Marshall II.

The robot was now equipped with new armor reminiscent of transparent, white ice. In its hands and on its head were cross-like blades that were made of blue ice.

Due to its replenished magic, the Marshall II's output was now greater than it had been when it was completely unharmed. Its appearance was reminiscent of an anthropomorphized church made of ice.

This was my Embryo.

The true form of Cocytus — a Type Maiden with Chariot.

"GRRROOAAAAGGHHHHHHH!"

Despite what had just transpired, Gouz didn't stop his charge.

That was the correct reaction. Not knowing hesitation or fear, Gouz was a perfect example of a true warrior.

He was strong, indeed.

But it was already over for him. The moment I'd decided to use Cocytus' power, Gouz had lost all chance of emerging victorious. It didn't matter how tough of a man-eater he was.

The stage was set.

The gates of hell were opening to welcome another sinner.

"Omnes relinquite spes, o vos intrantes."

After reciting the words etched onto the entrance to hell — "Abandon all hope, ye who enter here" — I activated the skill.

"La Porte de l'Enfer."

Moments later, Gouz's life reached a bitter end.

Paladin Ray Starling

The world of *Infinite Dendrogram* had a job system.

Just as I had my "Paladin" job, so did other Masters and tians have theirs. The only people who *didn't* have jobs were Masters who had just started *Infinite Dendrogram* and tian children.

Jobs were many and varied. Vanguard roles alone had job groupings such as Knight — which included my Paladin job — Swordsman, Warrior, Gladiator, Pugilist, Samurai, and so on.

Then there were job groupings for rearguard roles, support roles, crafting roles, et cetera... When summed up, they were just too many to properly grasp.

The catalog my brother had given me had the conditions for acquiring every low-rank and high-rank job. The entries there amounted to several thousands, and — naturally — I still had trouble remembering them all. The number of active Masters was several hundred thousand, and I had a feeling that — if jobs had been split evenly among them — there would've been fewer than one hundred people on each of them. Of course, the actual job distribution was nowhere near "even." Rook's Pimp job, for example, wasn't too popular among Masters.

There was no denying that the number of jobs available for people in other MMORPGS was incomparable to that of *Dendro*'s freedom. But despite this overwhelmingly great amount, there was one job that was etched into my mind. It was one I couldn't quite forget about.

It was a job named "Necromancer."

Its selling points were its many debuff skills, offensive dark magic skills...

...and, of course, Necromancy — the skill that allowed one to turn corpses into tamed monsters at the cost of MP.

It could be used on both people and creatures without any problems.

Of course, the difficulty of turning a corpse into a tamed monster depended on how powerful the creature was when alive.

On the other hand, that meant that children — being nearly powerless — could be turned into undead without much trouble.

The catalog said that one of the conditions to get the high-rank job of the Necromancer grouping was related to the number of successful uses of the Necromancy skill. I'd read on the wiki that some tian criminals were Necromancers who used children and the sickly to increase that counter for that very purpose. Some theorized that getting the Superior Job of this grouping involved a similar condition.

The implications of the idea made me sick, so I'd etched the existence of Necromancers into my memory. And now, it all came back to me.

Trying to make sense of why the Gouz-Maise Gang was kidnapping children, I made my way towards the end of the underground hallway.

$\Diamond$

It was a straight path without any branches, so all I had to do was go forward.

Although I didn't encounter any bandits, I had to face some undead — adults this time — blocking my way.

They'd probably been made from corpses that had gathered here when the fortress had still been occupied by the army. Then again, they could've just as well been the remains of the adventurers the bandits had defeated.

I destroyed each and every undead in my way. Even if they had been people once, I couldn't let them stop me. If I did, the dead would just keep piling up.

Finally, I reached the end of the hallway, where I was greeted by a door. A heavy-set thing of wood, secured by a steel padlock, it separated me from the room behind it, where I felt the presence of living creatures.

"Hhgh!"

I swung my Nemesis down on the door itself, rather than the padlock. As pieces of wood scattered all over, I jumped inside and examined the surroundings.

I was fully ready to cut down any gang members that were awaiting me, but the only living creatures here were caged children.

There was a total of seven of them.

From their closed eyes, I could tell that they were in deep sleep. I didn't know which, but I had little doubt that one of them was Roddie — the one we had to save. Of course, I fully intended to save them all, quest-related or not.

I found it a bit strange that the children seemed to be the only people here.

"Not a single gang member?" I said in confusion.

"This room had a padlock on it, after all," said Nemesis. "It might be fair to assume they left the child-watching to the undead."

"I guess that makes sense." I cautiously examined the children and the condition they were in. Reaching through the grates, I gently shook some of them, but they showed no signs of awakening.

"I assume they're either drugged or under the effect of some debuff spell," commented Nemesis.

"Probably," I nodded. It was just my intuition, but I believed it to be magic. After all, the one who'd done it was probably the one who'd made undead out of those children in the hallway.

To him, they were just cards to use to get ransom money. And if it didn't come, he'd readily kill them and use his Necromancy to desecrate their corpses. I was beyond disgusted.

"Master, look to the right," Nemesis said.

I looked, saw another door — an iron one this time. Upon approaching it, I lightly spun the doorknob. The way it felt made it obvious that it wasn't locked and that I'd have no trouble opening it.

"Will you go inside?" asked Nemesis.

"Of course," I replied.

I spun the doorknob and quickly kicked the door open. I had already broken one door. If there was someone in here, then there was no reason for me to act all stealthy.

"Is that a…?" I began.

The first thing I saw after entering was a person. A young boy, to be precise. He was sleeping — just like the children in the cages. In the middle of the room, on the floor under him, there was a highly detailed magic circle.

"There's a lot to be said about the tastes of the owner of this room." Nemesis' voice was steeped in anger.

The magic circle on the floor wasn't the only thing she was referring to. In fact, the magic circle was tame when compared to the rest of the scene.

Stains of blood covered both the walls and the ceiling. *Something's* leather was heaped against the edge of the room. A nearby barrel was overflowing with white bones. The table next to the wall was covered in utensils and materials, but nothing really stood out until I saw a taxidermy construction of a right hand with twenty fingers, which compelled me to shift my gaze away.

I silently suppressed my rage. There was no denying that we were standing in the laboratory of the Necromancer who'd created those undead.

However, the Necromancer himself was nowhere in sight. It was safe to assume that he'd gone out to face Hugo.

The child on the magic circle was probably going to be his next guinea pig. We'd saved him by coming here.

"What now?" asked Nemesis. "Should we ensure the children's safety or go help Hugo with the bandit elimination?"

That was a hard decision to make. Saving the children was our primary goal, but carrying all seven of them somewhere safe would be too difficult for me alone. However, if I left them here and went out to fight, I'd increase the possibility of them being used as hostages.

My other option was to stay here and protect the children while Hugo took care of the bandits, but it'd all go to hell if Hugo got killed.

"Man, this is a tough one…" I sighed.

"For now, I think you should take that youngling to the other room," said Nemesis. "I don't know what kind of magic circle that is, but I don't believe it's safe for a child to sleep on."

I nodded and moved towards the child in the circle.

After a few steps, I stepped on something that seemed strange. It was a particularly thick piece of cloth. At first glance, it looked like a thin mattress made of felt, but I soon noticed that it had a pair of sleeves sewn on it, making it clear that it was a piece of clothing — a robe, to be precise. What seemed strange wasn't the fact that clothing was lying on the ground, but the fact that I could feel something hard under it.

I kicked the robe away to find out what it was.

"These are…"

…bones — that was the source of the hard sensation beneath my feet.

Their presence didn't surprise me in the least. The nearby barrel was full of them, after all. However, I found it strange that half of the bones were those of a human, while the other half belonged to something else. The non-human bones were thicker and reminded me of a horse skeleton I'd seen in a museum once.

"How did human and horse bones end up lying in the same place?" I asked.

"I would guess they belong to a horse-man," said Nemesis. "As far as I am aware, this is just about how their skeletal remains look."

That reminded me that, back in Gideon, I had seen some members of a race that looked much like the centaurs from Greek myth.

I glanced back down at my feet. The upper body and skull bones clearly belonged to a human, while the bones that matched to the lower body seemed about the right fit for an equine. Indeed, there was little doubt that they belonged to a horse-man.

However, there were things to be said about their large size. I didn't know that race's average, but at the very least, it was clear that it didn't belong to a child.

How did the bones of a mature horse-man end up here? I thought.

"The Necromancer might've somehow gotten his hands on one of their corpses and used it in his experiments," said Nemesis.

"He would've cleaned it up if that was the case," I argued. "After all, he's already preparing his next guinea pig."

I looked at the child on the magic circle. It didn't take a genius to see that the Necromancer was fully ready for the next experiment. He wouldn't have left the bones from a previous experiment just lying on the floor like this.

I mean, the madman is methodical enough to put all the other bones in that barrel there, I thought.

"Trying to understand the thought process of a madman is a fool's errand, if you ask me," said Nemesis.

"…No point in considering it, huh?" I muttered.

She had a point. My prime objective was to move that child away from here.

After using Nemesis to shatter the magic circle multiple times and making sure that I wouldn't activate some strange magic, I stepped inside and picked the boy up.

Sleeping on the cold floor had made his body temperature drop. Still, he was breathing properly and had a stable pulse. Slightly relieved, I began carrying him on my back and made my way out of the room.

Suddenly, I felt his breath behind me.

That was normal — considering where he was — but for some reason, a chill arced down my spine like lightning…

"Die."

I was unsure of where that word came from. But it was too late. I heard the sound of a blade slicing my neck.

Somehow I'd missed it, but the child on my back had a dagger in his hands.

As my carotid artery began oozing blood, I fell to the cold, stony floor.

One of the two leaders of the Gouz-Maise Gang, Lich Maise
This world had a power most referred to as "Superior Jobs."

Out of the thousands of jobs available to humanoid creatures, those were the ultimate peak — available only to a select few.

Superior Jobs allowed people to surpass the limits of their corporeal form.

One of the people who had a Superior Job was the Arch Wiseman — the one they called the kingdom's guardian deity. His magic power was nothing short of divine. He could part the ground beneath and even bring down the heavens themselves.

However, in the war with Dryfe, the Arch Wiseman had been defeated by the King of Beasts — a Master and another owner of a Superior Job.

Though that had been nothing but a tragedy for the Kingdom of Altar, a number of people were glad that he was gone. After all — the throne of a Superior Job was exclusive to the one possessing it. With the kingdom's Arch Wiseman dying, the role of the Arch Wiseman became open for those wanting to take it.

I, too, was aiming for a Superior Job. However, it was a job completely unlike the Wiseman's.

The Superior Job I set my sights upon was at the apex of the Necromancer grouping. It was a job known as the King of Corpses.

Its power was far above the magic of common Necromancers... and beyond even the Necromancy of Liches — those who became undead themselves.

Anyone seated in the throne of corpses would be immortal, undying, and commanding power surpassing that of all the deceased. It was the only method to receive the undeath that only Masters had.

That was the King of Corpses.

I started leading the Gouz-Maise gang to further my efforts at getting this Superior Job. The kidnapped children were there to help me practice my Necromancy. The money was necessary for me to get certain magic items and to bribe Caldina.

In that country, money was the start and the end of the conversation. *Everything* in Caldina had a price. A sufficiently-greased palm could even get their army to act in response to movements from Gideon's soldiers.

Since this place was near the border, that made the kingdom hesitant to attack us because it could provoke Caldina.

Also, with all the Conceal and Presence Manipulation magic items I'd bought from them, the kidnapping of materials had become significantly easier. Blessed with abundant ingredients and the perfect environment, I was able to study the path of Necromancy to my heart's content and slowly made my way towards the throne of the King of Corpses.

Getting this Superior Job required the fulfillment of several difficult conditions and then passing a certain test. I had learned the conditions by deciphering an ancient text describing the secret processes.

The first condition there was "Turn 5,000 years' worth of life into death," which I'd easily achieved by making this fortress my hideout and having the gang work for me. Since I focused on children — who were both easy to convert into undead and still had long, happy futures ahead of them — it all went extremely smoothly. I needed fewer than a hundred of them for this, but since the undead were a great asset, I continued on doing it.

The second condition — which I'd achieved, as well — was the creation of a Crystal of Resentment. It was made by forcing enormous amounts of fear — or grudge, to be more precise — into a Crystal of Purity — an item that cleansed the corruption of the undead.

Gouz helped me a lot with this. The fear of the children he ate while they were still alive manifested in exquisite, sorrowful grudges.

Of course, the grudge I got from them when using the Anguish Circle to turn them into materials for the undead wasn't too bad, either.

The once-white crystal that had emitted an irritatingly divine light was now blackened to the very core.

With that, I'd had already fulfilled the conditions to become the King of Corpses. All that was left was going to Legendaria — the place where the job's throne was sealed — to clear the ordeal quest and make the title my own.

Both the fortress and the gang had outlived their use. Gideon would soon become crowded with some particularly pesky individuals. Before that happened, I planned to take Gouz — my only useful subordinate — with me, then destroy all the knowledge I might've left here and leave once and for all.

That was when a particularly reckless intruder sneaked into the fortress.

◆

"Die."

A moment after I spoke that word, I heard the sound of a man dropping to the laboratory floor. I couldn't see the look on his face, but the ground was drenched in his fresh blood.

Standing next to him was a child I'd magically controlled to slice open the man's throat.

An undead would've easily been recognized by the description over its head, I thought. *In such cases, it's better to use them alive.*

"So a child got you to let your guard down, huh?" I muttered. "What a fool you are."

I began rebuilding my scattered body. Once my horse-man skeleton came together, I re-equipped my robe. Then, skin and leather began covering my bones before expanding to fit the flesh inside.

A moment before, I had been nothing but bones, which was made possible by one of my Lich skills — Corpsification. To the man now lying on the ground, I'd probably looked like a standard set of skeletal remains.

I was undead and had Lich — a high-rank necromancer job — as my own. Having such trickery at my disposal was only natural.

"Oh? You're still alive?" I said while looking down at the man. Although he'd lost so much blood that the stream from his neck had significantly weakened, he still seemed to have a pulse. In his right hand, he held a black halberd with a flag trailing from behind. I tried identifying it, but didn't get any results. That could only mean one thing: the weapon was an Embryo and the man was a Master.

"You're still conscious, too?" I spoke again. "Well, it matters not. The dagger was coated in a Poison and Paralysis-causing fluid, specially concocted by yours truly. A Lich's poison is nothing to sniff at, either. You'll die without being able to do anything about it."

The Bleeding and Poison was draining his life, while Paralysis sealed all and any movement. Shame that he was a Master — I could've harvested a truly potent grudge from him if he hadn't been one.

Masters were a terrible source for grudges. When killed, they would simply come back to life three days later. Compared to tians, their fear of death and resentment towards their murderers was simply... mediocre. Not only that — their absolute immortality made them live as though everything was just a game.

That was exactly how the party of Masters that'd attacked this place had been. My magic and Gouz's strength had been more than enough to take care of them, but since I hadn't even been able to turn their corpses into undead, they'd been absolutely useless to my Necromancy work. Masters irked me to no end. Their treatment of this world as a plaything, and the fact that they automatically had immortality... the one thing I had decided to make my life's work.

...Oh, that made me remember. The first party to come here had been comprised entirely of tians, and the grudges I'd collected by torturing them had been simply superb. Ah, the fun I'd had back then. Their corpses had become some excellent materials, too.

Turning tians into undead was extremely easy. I was rather intrigued by the idea of making undead out of Masters, as well, but for now, I had to make due with merely getting rid of them whenever they intruded.

By now, Gouz had probably taken care of this man's ally on the surface. All I had to do now was leave the fortress, go where I must, complete the ordeal, and become the King of Corpses.

"With that in mind, it's time to move out and head towards Legendaria," I muttered.

As I made my way towards the laboratory door, I noticed the materials... the children I'd put to sleep in the other room. I'd nearly forgotten.

"The gang act is over," I said. "Better kill all the children and turn them into materials for my undea... hm?"

The moment I said that, I saw the fingers of the man on the ground twitch a little bit. That small action — combined with the look on the side of his face — made me realize something.

"Did you actually come all the way here just to save the children?" I asked. "It wasn't for my treasure?"

He didn't say a word. Not like he could, considering his current condition, but his reaction was more than enough.

"Hah... hah... HAHAHAHAHAHAHAHA!" I placed my hands on my belly and laughed out loud.

No other reaction was appropriate. How could I *not* laugh?

"Hahahahahah! An inhuman immortal? Going out of his way to save a few brats? Ghahahahahahah! Oh my, quite a heroic way to play you've found, Mister Master."

Thought you'd roleplay as some champion of justice, huh? I thought. The fact that *this* was where it had gotten him filled me with great bliss.

"Heheheh," I continued laughing. "All right, this is how it will go. I'll create some lovely little undead creatures, and you will watch it happen until the poison kills you. Who knows? You might learn something. After all, I'm quite skilled at it, if I say so myself. But that is only natural, considering that I've already created hundreds of them!"

In response to my words, the man on the ground exuded some horrific, traumatic emotions.

Excellent, I thought. *It appears that even a Master can be a good source when properly agitated. But even more than that, as one who will soon be the King of Corpses, I know now that I will thoroughly enjoy the freedom to look down on any and all immortal Masters.*

"Now, then..." I said. "The children with thick-looking bones will be turned into Skeletons, while all the others will do fine as Zombies. Oh, but it might be a good idea to turn these pretty-looking ones into taxidermy pieces and sell them off somewhere. Despite appearances, my hands are quite dexterous, so I'm actually pretty decent at managing the finer details. Some men of culture value my work quite highly."

In response, I got more angry silence.

Ah, the joy, I thought. *This is pure bliss.*

I'd never have expected to have this much fun with a Master. His sorrow was like the perfect seasoning.

However, it was time to end it.

"Now, let's start with the brat that cut your neck!" I exclaimed. "First, I'll have him cut his own neck and—"

Suddenly, a gust of wind...

...followed by the sound of something hitting the ground.

"...What?" Confused, I looked to where the sound came from and saw something very familiar.

It was a left hand, covered in magic rings. Magic rings that had cost me a fortune.

Isn't that... my own left hand? I thought, stunned.

"If you... are..."

The man whose defeat was all but certain slowly spoke up. His right arm was raised in the air.

"If you... are not among the living..."

The blade of the halberd he held was emitting a noble, white gleam. I recognized it. It was imbued with the bane of the undead — Purifying Silverlight.

"If you... lost sight of what it means to be a person..."

He slowly stood up and faced towards me. The neck wound that was surely there less than a minute ago had disappeared without a trace.

"If you... are the one responsible for *that* scene..."

His expression had neither the weariness of Poison, nor the heaviness of Paralysis.

"If you... claim that you will keep on doing it..."

The only real emotion on his face was in the light in his eyes — a blaze of pure rage.

"...then I *will* kill you."

It was the first time I had seen a Master — one of those immortal, inhuman beasts of undeath — make such an expression.

I couldn't articulate it completely, but what I felt was dread. Utter and unmatched dread.

My instincts were screaming, telling me only one thing:

Run! He is going to extinguish you.

"■ ■ ■ ■ — Abyssal Delusion!"

Dead Man's Bind!

I quickly used the most vile hexes I had at my disposal. They were two high-rank debuff spells — one was vocal and came accompanied by a chant, while the other came from the magic item on my right hand and didn't need any words.

Abyssal Delusion was a powerful hex that gave the affected the Death Sentence, Weakness, and Deterioration status effects, making them rot and become corpses while still alive. Dead Man's Bind was another spell with three debuffs — Binding, Curse, and Lethargy. Together, they gave a total of six particularly powerful status effects.

This combination had sent many of my enemies to their deaths. Anyone unlucky enough to receive it was rendered completely immobile.

"Ghaah!"

Yet *he* didn't stop. As though he'd reversed the effects of my hexes, he became more intimidating and horizontally swung his halberd — shining with Purifying Silverlight — towards me.

"Guh?!" I exclaimed. If I had been but a step closer, his attack would've split my torso.

I couldn't let that happen. Taking fatal damage from *him* was something I had to avoid at all costs.

I was a Lich — an undead master of magic. Most of my wounds would mend a moment after they'd happened. I could lose an arm or get my body split in half — no such damage was critical to me.

However, in this case, the mending didn't work at all. In fact, the arm he'd cut off had already turned to dust.

That was only natural. After all — he was wielding Purifying Silverlight. It was a gleam used only by a limited number of Paladins and Temple Knights — a light meant for the sole purpose of purging the undead. No matter how great of a Lich I was, I couldn't come back from a fatal attack by a weapon blessed with that loathsome shine.

The fear of death overwhelmed me. It was a feeling that had become alien to me over time. It was a feeling that would never again strike me once I became the King of Corpses. But here and now, it was raw. It shook my very being.

"Awaken Undead!" Using my Necromancy, I activated the undead monsters I'd stored in the barrel in this room.

Countless Skeleton Soldiers answered my call.

However, they meant little.

There was no chance of them winning against this *aberration*, but it mattered not. They only had to buy the time I needed to run away.

As the undead began charging at him, I turned around and left the laboratory. If I stayed any longer, I knew it would become my grave.

Then — as my breath became ragged — I ran towards the surface through the underground hallway. Once we Liches became undead, our hearts and lungs ceased their function and were replaced by a gathering of crystallized magic. Thus, physical lack of breath was something I should never have experienced again. And yet, I felt as though I was suffocating.

"Why is a Master...?!" Through my ragged breath, I voiced my dread. "Why is one of those immortal abominations... *actually furious*?"

This fear was unknown to me. The fear of *that thing's* emotion. The terror I felt towards that aberration.

Terror — that was the word. Having one of those abominations direct such pure killing intent and rage towards me was nothing short of terrifying. After all, that meant that an immortal, indestructible animal would be hunting me for all eternity.

I had to escape. Anywhere near that aberration was certain death, so I had to leave this fortress and run where he could never find me.

I had to do it — and I *could* do it.

Though I was a Lich, my Agility was greater than his, so it would be perfectly possible for me to distance myself from him.

Reaching the surface would mean regrouping with Gouz. Then, I'd simply have to make him fight the abomination while I made my escape.

"I can do it…!" Picturing that future made me relieved.

Due to me being a horse-man, the underground hallway's soundscape was dominated by the sound of my horse legs hitting the floor.

However, the sound soon mingled with another.

"…What?" I burst out.

Its source was approaching me from behind. Systematic, yet rough impacts on the ground — the sound was exactly the same as the ones coming from under my feet. It was the sound of a galloping horse.

"Gh…!"

Unable to bear the tension caused by the approaching sound, I turned around.

What I saw was far beyond my imagination. It was an artificial, silver horse, speeding through the underground hallway. And to the side of it was the abomination.

For some reason, he wasn't riding it. The aberration was holding the silver horse's reins with his right hand, scraping his leg armor across the ground. It was reminiscent of a Granvaloan water sport.

In his left hand, he was still holding the halberd as the flag flowing out of it fluttered wildly in the air.

Why isn't he using his Riding skill? I thought.

That way of riding it should soon break his legs and render them useless, right? But why doesn't it look like he's taking any damage?

The strange sight left me with several questions, but their answers didn't matter.

What mattered was the fact that he was still chasing me… and that the horse was faster than me, meaning that he would soon catch up.

"AAAAUUUGHHHHHHHH!"

Disregarding my shame and reputation, I screamed in fear while running towards the surface as fast as I could.

On the surface, I would meet up with Gouz. He could buy me all the time I needed to run away.

"Awaken… AWAKEN UNDEAAAAD!" Not slowing down whatsoever, I activated the undead monsters I had buried in the walls for emergencies such as these.

They were called "High-End Skeleton Warriors." I had made these high-rank undead by using the corpses of skilled tians. They were the remains of the party Gouz and I had taken care of.

Six High-End Skeleton Warriors stood between me and him. Though turned undead, they had all been owners of high-rank jobs once, so there was a chance that...

"Out of our way!" two voices — his and another, feminine one — said that at the same time. A moment later, the mass of silver went through the Skeletons and returned them all to dust.

The halberd in his left hand and the hooves of the man-made horse ended my undead in a blink of an eye. I then noticed that not just the halberd, but the entire body of the steed was shining with the Silverlight.

"Aaagh?!"

That was no living horse — it was a piece of equipment. Emitting the Silverlight and galloping at a great speed, it pulverized all and any undead that touched it.

It didn't matter if the undead were high-rank. The thing was the bane of *all* undead. It was a silver bullet that brought forth the ultimate end.

"GGGHAAAHHHHH!"

Completely desperate, I used the moment my undead monsters had bought me to climb up the stairs leading to the surface. With the Master being dragged by the horse, he couldn't get up the stairs properly. It ought to affect his speed.

A moment before he could catch up, I ran up the stairs and escaped to the surface.

"GOUZ! GOOUUUZ!" I screamed while dashing through the fortress.

Once I ran through the hallway on the first floor and could see the gates of the fortress, I was overcome with relief. That was because I saw Gouz's face.

A moment later, that relief changed into despair.

That was because Gouz's face… was the only thing there.

I couldn't grasp what had happened, but Gouz's dismembered head — completely frozen — was impaled on the gate.

Wh-Where did his brawny body go? I asked myself. It was nowhere in sight. All I could see were pieces of frozen meat, scattered all over the area outside the gate. Two of those pieces — placed close to each other — looked much like Gouz's feet.

Right next to them stood an anomaly looking much like an anthropomorphized church made of ice — an enemy of my kind if I ever saw one.

"Choose your fate, sinner," spoke the anomaly. "Which end do you desire? Hell, or Divine Retribution?"

I instantly understood what it was talking about.

It was telling me to choose to meet my end, either at the hands of the icy anomaly or the silver aberration.

"No!" I shouted. "This is not happening!"

I can't die here! I've come so far! And now, when the throne of the King of Corpses is within arms reach, I…

"Why…?!" I voiced my despair yet again. "What…?!"

What did I do to deserve this?!

"Very well," the anomaly spoke again. "Divine punishment it is."

It then pointed an icy blade towards something behind me.

I turned around and saw the silver aberration.

The abomination had caught up with me.

A sound thick with dread escaped my mouth. I could no longer run or hide.

Th-There must be something I can do! I thought. *Don't I have a teleportation magic item on me? No?! I should have something! I just…!*

"Huh…?" As I dug through the inventory in my robe, my fingers touched something that made me gasp. I slowly took it out. It was a pitch black, crystalline object that emitted no light whatsoever — a Crystal of Resentment.

"No…" I said in despair. I held the obsidian-like object in my hand. It was an item without which I had no hope of becoming the King of Corpses. Creating it had required me to lead the Gouz-Maise Gang and spend nearly a year sacrificing a great number of children.

However, aside from being the condition for becoming the King of Corpses, the crystal was also the ultimate medium for the Necromancer grouping's magic. Using it here was painful, but…

"If I die… it will have all been for naught!" I screamed.

I had to pick between dying and using the Crystal to survive, so I gladly picked the latter. If I didn't, the time and effort I'd dedicated to my cause would've all gone to waste. I simply had to survive and do it all over again in some other town. After all — the time, the work I was willing to dedicate and the sacrifices were endless.

As long as I'm alive, I can restart as many times as I have to! I thought. *Indeed — I cannot let myself die here! Dying to this accidental encounter is unacceptable!*

"YOU DISGUSTING, MONSTROUS CURS!" I roared while filling the Crystal of Resentment — my greatest treasure — with great amounts of magic. **"YOU MONSTERS WILL NOT TAKE MY LIFE FROM ME!"**

After reforming the wicked feelings within the crystal to pure destructive energy, I released it all towards the abomination, fully aware that it would destroy the fortress, as well. After all, it was the strongest offensive magic skill any Lich could have.

"DEADLY MIXEEERRRR!"

With great dread and frenzy overwhelming me, I unleashed the most powerful attack I'd ever cast. It was great enough to instantly eradicate a Pure-Dragon. There was simply no way for him to survive it.

"Counter Absorption."

And yet...

"Ah...? Ugh...? Eahhh...?" Confusion escaped my mouth in the form of strange sounds. The magic I'd dedicated my entire being to was blocked by a barrier of light he created before it. "Th-This cannot be!"

The shock made me lose my footing and fall to the ground. A moment later, the abomination was right in front of me.

"Ghah?! N-No!"

The moment I attempted to stand up and run away in fear, his halberd — still emitting a silver gleam — penetrated my torso and pinned me to the spot.

"GYYAAAHH!"

I was unable to move — both due to the halberd piercing me and the pain caused by Silverlight — and the aberration stood before me.

"Stop... running," it hissed through its ragged breath.

"W-Wait!" I said. "I won't run! You caught me!"

Escape was impossible at this point, but I still had to survive, even if it meant begging for my life.

"L-Let's make a deal!" I spoke in a panic. "M-Money! I'll give you money! I still have lots of it! 70,000,000 lir, to be precise! It's yours! Take it all, but please, let me go!"

The aberration said nothing.

Yes! I thought. *He reacted to my offer! I don't care if I have to give him all my coins! I have already sacrificed my Crystal of Resentment! Money is a small price to pay for survival!*

"Hhaaahh…" He sighed and extended his right palm towards me.

Excellent! It worked!

"Khah! Hahahah!" I laughed. "G-Give me a moment. I'll just take it all out of the inventory, so—"

"Your life is payment enough," he said, cutting my words short.

"Eh?"

As confusion overtook me, his open hand changed into a fist, and the bracer on it began to emit that painfully-familiar silver light.

I heard my own skull crack and squelch. And then I was gone.

Paladin Ray Starling

The headless corpse of the Lich became dust and began to crumble.

At the same time, my body quickly became too heavy for me to stand properly and I dropped to the ground before I could do anything to soften my fall.

"Looks like… it's over," I forced out a mutter. My status window displayed Poison, Paralysis, Death Sentence, Weakness,

Deterioration, and a number of other debuffs. There were so many that keeping track of them all seemed like a fool's errand.

However, the fact that the status effects I'd gotten from my opponent had come back left me with no doubt that he was defeated.

"Like a Flag Flying the Reversal." That was the unique skill that Nemesis had gained with her second form — The Flag Halberd. It reversed all the debuffs given to me by hostile creatures. On the flip side, that meant that it would stop the moment the relevant hostiles were dead. The return of his debuffs was the ultimate proof of his death.

The moment after he'd manipulated the child into slicing my neck, I'd made Nemesis go from her greatsword form into The Flag Halberd and activated the Reversal. Thus my reaction to the debuffs displayed in my status window. Once the skill was active, Bleeding began to increase my bloodflow, Poison healed me, and Paralysis upped my physical abilities.

The damage I'd gotten from the surprise attack had been healed by the reversed Poison while I was still on the ground. Once that effect had closed the wound on my neck, the Bleeding status effect had completely disappeared.

Later, when he'd hit me with those debuff spells, I'd turned them all into buffs, as well. Though I'd felt that some of them didn't seem like they got reversed, it was clear that I was under no negative effects.

He'd ended up greatly buffing me and reversing the power balance.

He'd also had the problem of compatibility. The Purifying Silverlight was a skill meant for purging undead, and that was exactly what a Lich was. Also, Silver had been a great help in catching up to him when he'd run away.

Of course, I still didn't have the Riding skill. So I hadn't been *riding* him, per se. I'd merely let Silver gallop towards the Lich while I held on to him, letting my feet get dragged along the floor.

It hadn't been too different from one of those generic Western flick scenes where people got pulled around while tied to horses. In that state, my feet had gotten continuously damaged, but I'd been able to cover it with the healing from the reversed Poison.

Once on the surface, I'd blocked his final spell with Counter Absorption. Though it was far more powerful than Gardranda's flames, we had somehow been able to handle it.

For a moment, I'd thought the debuffs would make me collapse, but after the attack had been done, Nemesis had quickly changed back to The Flag Halberd and re-activated the Reversal, letting me come out of it unscathed. Then I'd pinned him down with my weapon and ended his life with my fist.

This whole battle had been extremely dangerous to me. I had only managed due to the convergence of several very specific circumstances. This wasn't a feat I'd be repeating any time soon.

"...I got really lucky here," I said.

"I know all the reasons why we emerged victorious, but even I can't help but think the same," Nemesis agreed.

Perhaps fate itself helped me hunt down and punish the scumbag who toyed with the lives of countless children, I thought.

I silently looked at my hand. The sensation I'd felt when I'd pulverized his head was still there. Either due to him being undead or because of my Silverlight, it had felt much like shattering a withered tree, but it'd been there nonetheless.

Though he was a piece of filth beyond any redemption, he was also the first tian I'd killed.

If I — being a Maiden's Master — felt as strongly about this world as I did about reality, this killing might cause me pain.

"I have nothing against such considerations, but you should leave it for later," said Nemesis.

"Nemesis?" I asked, slightly puzzled. She had already returned to her human form and was looking down at me.

She pointed at one part of the status window — specifically, the Death Sentence debuff. Upon further inspection, I noticed that it had a counter next to it, saying "362 seconds."

Is this one of those debuffs that kills you when the counter reaches 0? I thought.

"So, Master, do you happen to have any anti-debuff medicine?" she asked.

"I've got some Antidotes for poisons, but I never expected to get a debuff like *this*," I said.

This is bad… Really bad. At this rate, I'll get the death penalty.

Hugo was here, the children were safe, and the gang was eliminated, so I didn't have to worry about any of that. However, dying would mean missing the time we'd agreed on with Marie. I didn't like that scenario at all.

"Curse you, you wretched horse zombie!" shouted Nemesis. "You just *had* to leave us with this parting gift!"

"…Crap," I muttered. Due to all the debuffs on me, only my mouth worked properly, so I couldn't even hold my head in despair.

Nemesis began rummaging through my inventory to see if I had something that could help me. Silver — who I still hadn't called back — was looking down at me in a somewhat worried manner.

"You should drink this." Something hard was pushed against my jaw.

I looked and saw Hugo — who'd just jumped out of... what I could only describe as a see-through ice robot with a Magingear inside — pushing a potion against my mouth.

Once I gulped down the contents, my body became so light that it felt as though the debuffs were never there.

He followed it up with another potion. Once I drank that one, I looked at the status window and saw that all the status effects were gone.

"I'm healed!" I cried.

"Indeed you are!" said Nemesis. "You have our thanks, Hugo!"

"You're welcome," he smiled.

"What was this medicine, anyway?" I asked.

"An Elixir and a curse-removing High Spirit Water," he said.

"And you didn't mind giving them to me?" I asked.

"Not at all. After all, they came out of the inventory of the one I defeated." Hugo pointed at the ox head hanging on the gate.

I looked at that general direction and saw a number of items lying around the remains.

Some of them were bottles, just like the one I'd just drunk from.

"Why are the items scattered like that?" I asked.

"His inventory broke with my attack," answered Hugo. "I, uh... might've overdone it."

That made me remember the tutorial, when Cheshire had said that *this* was just about what happened when an inventory shattered. Though the power of the release often left the contents break, it was the easiest way to take the possessions of others. Due to that, some bad guys chose to attack rich people and spread their items all over the place.

The other ways to take someone's items were the Bandit grouping's Steal skill — which directly stole the items from people's inventories — and the Burglar grouping's Plunder skill — which switched the ownership of the taken items to the user. When I'd learned that, I had wondered why these two skills were in different job groupings despite not being *that* different.

"Hm? Is that a…?"

I noticed the inventory of the Lich I'd defeated peeking out from under his robe. While mine had the shape of a bag, his was a black, cube-like box.

In his last moments, he had been reaching into it to take his money and buy me off. So, by breaking that, I could probably get the money and some of the rare items he owned, but…

"I don't feel like touching the stuff left behind by that freak," I said.

His life was more than enough for me. Also, it was easy for me to imagine how he'd come to have those riches, and that didn't make them look attractive at all.

"I share the sentiment," said Nemesis. "That money is so dirty that simply picking it up might sully our hearts."

"I understand," said Hugo. "Feel free to leave it there, then. Someone will come across and take it eventually."

"True," I nodded.

Though, with the defeat of the Gouz-Maise Gang, this fortress was now as abandoned as it had been before they'd made it their hideout. It was uncertain if anyone would ever set foot here again.

Then again, reporting this event to the Adventurers' Guild would probably cause them to launch an investigation. It might be a good idea to tell them to gather any treasure the scumbags had left behind. Perhaps the money would become cleaner if it was used for the good of society... and those who'd suffered due to the gang's vile deeds.

"Oh yeah, Hugo," I said. That thought reminded me of something. "I encountered some kidnapped children in the dungeon. Eight of them are still alive. From what I can tell, they've been put to sleep via magic. I'd like us to band up and carry them outside, so... Wait, where's Cyco?"

We were done with everything here, and yet she was nowhere in sight.

I recall her leaving her party slot before the battle began, but she wasn't showing up at all anymore, so... did she get the death penalty?

"Cyco's fine," said Hugo. "Give me a moment. Cyco, come here... Yeah, it's fine."

He said that while facing the Magingear clad in armor that looked much like an icy church. A moment later, the armor scattered into countless white and blue light particles.

Without the frozen armor, the Magingear collapsed, making Hugo say something about getting a spare one from some "leader." However, Nemesis and I were more interested in where the light particles were heading. They all gathered in one spot and took a humanoid form.

"Hellooo."

It was the Master clad in white — Cyco. However, she no longer had the proof of Masterhood — the crest on her left hand.

Also, the way she'd changed shape was like a differently-colored version of Nemesis' shapeshifting.

"I see," said Nemesis. "So Cyco and I... are birds of a feather."

"Yes," she nodded. "My real name is Cocytus."

"Birds of a feather...?" I raised an eyebrow. "So she's actually a..."

...Type Maiden Embryo — the same as Nemesis. And Hugo was her Master.

"But didn't she have a crest on her left hand before?" I asked.

"It was there because of Crest Disguise — a skill unique to Type Maiden Embryos," answered Hugo. "It makes their hands and status displays look like those of a Master."

"I had no idea such a skill existed..." I said, slightly surprised.

"They get it after a while of fighting in their human forms," he said.

During my entire play time, I had yet to let Nemesis fight on her own. Obviously, I didn't have it.

"What use is that skill, anyway?" I asked.

"You'd be surprised," said Hugo. "Due to them being unique and unpredictable, Embryos are powerful wild cards. With Crest Disguise, you can make it seem like there are more Masters — and thus, Embryos — than it appears."

So you can use it for bluffing, huh? I thought. *I feel like it might have other uses, too, so perhaps we should learn that skill ourselves.*

"Anyway, now that we're all here, we should go to the dungeon and take the children back to the light of day," I said.

"Agreed," nodded Hugo.

Nemesis, Hugo, Cyco, and I all began making our way towards the fortress' dungeon.

With there being four of us and with me having Silver, there was a chance that we could take them all in one trip. Also, with the Lich being dead, the children might've woken up from his spell, so we had to hurry up and calm them down.

The surroundings of the abandoned fortress.

"…Are they gone?" a voice asked.

"Yeah, they went in the fortress."

In the forest surrounding the abandoned fortress, in an area that had even denser foliage than the route taken by Hugo's Marshall II, there were five suspicious-looking men.

"I didn't expect the bosses to get beaten," said one of them.

These were the remnants of the Gouz-Maise Gang, and the very same five men that Ray and Hugo had encountered back in Gideon.

After Ray and Cyco had beaten them up and handed them over to the guards, some of their allies had jumped out and rescued them before they could be jailed.

After that, they'd followed the gang's carriages from a considerable distance — just to make sure that they weren't followed — and when they'd reached the fortress, they'd found their hideout and fellow gang members being completely destroyed.

They'd been lucky that they were in a place where Cyco's Enemy Detect skill couldn't reach them. Thus, they'd been able to hide it out and survive the massacre.

"What now?" asked one of them.

"What do you mean, 'what' — we're getting outta here!" answered another. "We can't do shit against monsters that can kill our bosses, who were pretty damn monster-like themselves."

"Crap, that means that we have to leave all the treasure behind." One of the men — specifically, the one that'd gotten punched by Ray — clicked his tongue in frustration. "...Oh, wait." He seemed to have just gotten an idea. "Yeah, *that's* what we should do!"

He nodded, completely satisfied with himself.

"The hell's got into you?" The other men looked at him, completely confused.

"They're in the fortress now, right?" he spoke up. "So it's a good time for us to take all the money and items the bosses left behind! Also, we can easily take the brats in them carriages there. We can use them to get the ransom money or just sell them somewhere in Caldina. Or maybe we can buy our way into some other local gangs!"

"Oh, man!" another man cried.

"That's an idea I can get behind!"

Their fellow gang member's suggestion made the other men turn joyous.

"There's no better time than now, then..." said one.

"Yeah!" howled another. "Let's get the items and the brats and get the hell out!"

They then split up. Some began gathering the items, while the others linked the living horses to the carriages with the children.

However, one of them — the one that'd suggested that they do what they were doing — was tilting his head near Maise's corpse, which was nothing but dust now.

"What's up with you?" asked another man.

"Boss Maise's inventory isn't broken," he answered. It was the very same inventory that Ray and Hugo had decided not to break.

"Huuhh? Break it, then, retard," the other man said. "All of us who had Plunder have already croaked, so that's the only thing we can do here."

As was natural for a band of brigands, the gang had people with Steal and Plunder skills. However, all of them had died to Hugo's Marshall II.

"True that," the man nodded. "Guess I'll do just that, then."

The man took out a dagger and — with great force — pierced through the inventory. Naturally, it broke and released its contents all over the area.

"Whooaaaahhhh! Get a load of all these coins!"

"Seriously! I don't think we even have to be bandits anymore! We can live like nobles with this!"

"We have the brats, too, so maybe we should start being Slave Dealers!"

"Good idea!"

The money Maise had left behind made them all imagine a bright future. They were surrounded by great riches. Just as Maise had said to Ray, the amount he'd had on him was over 70,000,000 lir. Of course, there were many rare gems, equipment pieces, and materials, as well.

With all of this, they could easily make all their dreams come true. Their futures would become even more secure after the next step. Every man was thinking it at this point. Every man wanted to kill the others and make all of the riches their exclusive property.

However... that was completely impossible.

"Huh?" one spoke in confusion. "What's this?"

He picked up an item that was lying on the ground. From its outline alone, it looked much like a hen's egg. However, it was dark red in color and had a single area on it that looked much like an eyelid.

At first glance, it didn't look too different from the materials owned by Maise the Lich, but the man holding it wouldn't have said the same.

He had a high level Identification skill and could identify just about every item he came across, but he didn't get any results for the egg-like object. It confused him, for he'd never had any problems identifying materials or monster eggs. However, it was obvious that he couldn't see what the thing in his hand was. After all, it wasn't an item, a monster, or any other living creature, for that matter.

It was nothing but a *curse*.

"Awakening."

A voice rang out from every inch of the shell as the egg opened its "eyelid."

"Eee!"

It surprised the man into attempting to throw it away, but the egg seemed to be stuck to his fingers like a strong vacuum.

"What?"

"What's wrong?"

The other men called out to the one who'd screamed — their faces still grinning due to the great amount of coin in their hands.

If they'd had the mind to realize that something was wrong and run away, the man with the egg in his hand would've been the only one to die.

However, that was hopeless. Anyone with that amount of sensitivity to danger would've never touched the belongings of Maise in the first place.

Maise had been among the greatest users of Necromancy in the Kingdom of Altar. Not only was he extremely thorough in his work towards becoming the King of Corpses — he was also a man who made use of people in a way most couldn't fathom.

He was the type of person to discard his most precious Crystal of Resentment — a necessity in becoming the King of Corpses — just to survive. He also hadn't hesitated to try prolonging his life by trying to buy off Ray with all the riches he'd amassed.

If a man with such an attachment to life were to be killed and had his treasure taken away...

Just what would he do?

Just how far would he go?

The men were defeated the moment they didn't consider those questions.

"Destruction of inventory: confirmed," said the egg. "Search: Lich Maise's Magical Wavelength... No response. Termination of Lich Maise: Confirmed. Assumption: plundering by hostiles. Invoking final spell — Undead Grudge Construction."

Once the voice had finished speaking, the fingers of the man touching the egg were sucked into it. Much like sewage going down a drain, his body began falling *into* the egg, his body cracking and spurting out blood as his form was compressed.

"AUGH!! UuGgh!! EeuGH!!"

Leaving only his completely inhuman screams, the thing that was once a man disappeared into the object.

The egg gained in size, becoming about as large as the egg of an ostrich.

"EEEEEK!"

"WH-WHAT THE HELL?!"

The spectacle made the other men panic, and they turned around and attempted to run away.

A moment later, the egg released pipes reminiscent of blood vessels and forced them into the backs of three out of four men that tried to escape. And — as if drinking juice through a straw — the egg began sucking the men into itself.

"GHHHY! JAUHGHH! EIHH!"

"EGGH… UGHAAAHH!!"

"ASSHHDIEDEAAAGAUGHH!!!"

Experiencing pain beyond their imagination, the men disappeared while speaking words that didn't belong in the realm of the sane.

"AAAAAHHHHH!"

The only survivor — the one who'd suggested they take the riches to begin with — dropped to the ground in fear and tried backing away while wetting himself. He thought the egg would launch a pipe at him, as well, but for some reason, it didn't happen. Instead, the egg began extending pipes towards the corpses surrounding the area.

The remains were numerous. All of them belonged to the Gouz-Maise Gang members who'd lost their lives in the battle against the Marshall II. The pipes reached into the pieces of meat scattered by cannon shots, the body halves split by knives, the corpses crushed by the robot's frame, and the head of Gouz hanging on the gate.

That wasn't all — the egg's surface also grew a funnel-like organ that began absorbing something invisible — *the grudges* — from both the air and the ground beneath. And — though his body had already become dust — that also included the regrets, hatred, and sorrow of Maise the Lich. All the flesh and grudge it'd gathered made the egg expand once more.

It was now an orb that seemed to mix the size of a gas tank and the fragility of a balloon. The scene before his eyes put the last survivor of the Gouz-Maise Gang into a complete stupor.

Soon enough, the orb cracked.

A moment later, it broke and birthed a beast too foul. A beast too hideous.

It was the ultimate result of the Gouz-Maise Gang and all they had done.

It wouldn't have been an exaggeration to say that this creature — this gathering of villainous flesh and emotion — was like a being straight out of hell. The corpses of hundreds were linked together like a jigsaw puzzle, forming the shape of an ox-headed horse-man.

Instead of blood, the only thing flowing through its veins was ill will, malicious grudges.

The gathering of the deceased showed nothing but disdain for all living creatures and moved only with the dark intention to make the whole world as dead as they were.

And, of course, the first target of its grudge was...

"Ah... Eh... Aahh?" ...the last survivor of the Gouz-Maise Gang.

The abomination's cadaverous hands grabbed hold of the man. Then it switched to holding him by the arms — with only its thumbs and index fingers — before beginning to pull on them. The action was so slow that it almost seemed gentle.

"AGH! AAGHYAAAAAHHHH!"

Slowly, surely... like a child toying with an insect... it continued pulling until one of the man's arms was torn from his body. Then it did exactly the same with the legs. And when the man was left with only one limb, the ox-headed horse-man opened its large mouth.

Though the pain he was in drove the man to the edge of insanity, he still had enough mind to understand why the creature was doing what it did. After all, he'd seen it happen many times during his days with the Gouz-Maise Gang.

"Ahaha... am I the... dessert...?"

Torn apart like an insect, the man was finally pulled into the ox's mouth and crushed by the countless, lethal fangs there.

And so, the Gouz-Maise Gang became one. Literally as one, they all composed a single being of hatred.

While the metaphorical sense might've been noble and grand, what was actually happening here was nothing short of vomit-inducing.

It was the birth of the most hideous undead.

[Non-player announcement]

[Discovered a monster that meets the conditions to be recognized as a Unique Boss Monster]
[Confirmed that no similar specimens have existed prior]
[Informed the control AI managing UBMs]

[Received approval from the control AI managing UBMs]
[Recognizing target as UBM]
[Strengthening the target's ability and providing it with the upon-death special reward function]
[Granting the target Epic status. Granting the target the name of "Revenant Ox-Horse, Gouz-Maise"]

Chapter Five > Revenant Ox-Horse

Paladin Ray Starling

The children had already woken up by the time we got to the dungeon, likely because the Lich had fallen.

At first, they thought we were with the bandits. They began to cry with fear, but thanks to Cyco and Nemesis calming them down, they soon believed that we wouldn't harm them.

As it turned out, Roddie — the child our quest requested us to save — was the very same boy that'd slit my throat back in the lab. He had no memory of ever being controlled, so I didn't see the need to bring it up.

When we were about to take the children back to the surface, I saw Hugo — who'd been looking around the lab — inquisitively examine the documents he'd found on the table there.

"Research on grudge, the Crystal of Resentment... and that's not all," he said. "It looks like he'd been studying the means of creating a Flesh Golem that uses grudge as its power source. Heh, reminds me of that one prototype we had. I guess people thinking the exact same thing exist everywhere in this world. Though I'd never have expected anyone to create something like this completely on their own... It's both impressive and horrific at the same time."

He put the documents he'd been examining into his inventory.

"What are those, Hugo?" I asked.

"Oh, just the research papers left behind by the Lich who made this fortress his hideout — Maise or whatever he was called. The concept is similar to the one behind a robot our clan was researching a while back, so I decided to take it to them. You know — as a souvenir."

"A robot?" I asked. "What does grudge have to do with that?"

"Let's go. I'll explain on the way."

We began walking out of the dungeon, and I was instantly met with a certain problem. Because they had been sleeping for so long, some of the children had become weak, rendering them unable to walk properly. Due to that, we had them ride Silver or carried them on our backs, but...

"Woof woof! Woof woof!" one of the kids cried.

Yep, I still have the dog ears, I thought. *And the kids just can't stop playing with them.*

"Me next! Me next!"

"No, me!"

I'm not sure how I feel about this popularity.

The relatively lively children were pestering me for a piggyback ride just so they could reach the dog ears.

"Looks like they're a big hit," smiled Hugo.

"...Good to see they're useful for *something*," I replied.

But man, they sure last a long time, I thought. Flamingo had told me they'd be gone by sunset, but it was already evening and they still didn't show any signs of disappearing.

"How curious," said Nemesis. "The lack of the Horse Riding skill made you fall down the first time you got on, yet these younglings can ride without any problem."

Getting the children out of the dungeon was a task that needed more people, so Nemesis was in her human form. She held Silver's reins as he was strutting forward like a pony.

Since it was unlikely that they had the Horse Riding skill, I was wondering about that, too. I could only assume that making Silver run while riding and simply leading him by holding the reins were completely different things.

"Okay," I spoke up. "So tell me about this thing about grudge and robots."

"All right," nodded Hugo. "The clan I'm in is focused mainly on crafting, and our current main products are Magingears. In fact, the Marshall II — Dryfe's official mass-produced machine — started out as an original item made by us."

That robot was actually built from scratch? I thought.

"Since Marshall II's completion, we've been developing new models, variation models, and better-armed models, but recently, we've been making plans to merge it with other crafts," he went on. "One of those plans focuses on the creation of a machine that uses dead people's grudge as a power source."

"Well, that sure doesn't sound good," I commented. "Why did that plan even exist?"

"Because all of Dryfe's machines — not just the Magingears — are huge MP sinks," he answered. "Replacing that MP with grudge would allow us to operate for longer and simplify the usage of stronger weaponry. That's the grudge power plan."

"How can grudge become power, anyway?" I asked.

"Heh," Hugo grinned. "You saw the answer to that just a few minutes ago, didn't you?"

I did? What does he mean?

"The last magic skill used by the Lich — Deadly Mixer."

"Oh, that," I said.

That attack had been immensely powerful. If I hadn't blocked it with Counter Absorption, I'd have vanished along with the fortress. In fact, the skill was even stronger than Figaro's chains. It was just that Counter Absorption was tougher now, due to Nemesis being in her second form, so the attack this time just barely hadn't been strong enough to break through it.

"That was a vile skill that turns grudge into destructive physical power and releases it at the target," Hugo continued. "Our craftsmen thought that — provided it was released on a smaller scale and handled more carefully — the same power could be used to power our engines. After all, this world already has Living Armor, which move due to the souls of the dead haunting it."

Living Armor, huh? I thought. *A not-too-uncommon monster type in fantasy RPGs.*

"One of our members said, 'If this goes well, we might create a weapon that absorbs the grudge permeating the battlefields and stays active semi-permanently,'" Hugo quoted. "Our clan was intrigued by the idea, so we got the help of a famous Master from the Necromancer grouping and began researching the utilization of grudge power, but…"

Hugo suddenly stopped talking, making me instantly understand how it must've gone down.

"It failed, huh?" I said.

"And how." He nodded. "The prototype was a failure that was both hard to control and had a tendency to go on a rampage. I helped with its disassembly and disposal. It happened back when I was still leveling up my Mechanic job."

"So, you're saying that the Lich... Maise had the same thing in his research paper?" I asked.

"Not at all," he said. "Though modified, the thing we at The Triangle of Wisdom were trying to build was but a machine weapon, while this is more along the lines of a Flesh Golem."

Flesh Golems were exactly what it said in the name — golems made of joined human or animal flesh. They were common in the more grotesque RPGs.

Now that I think about it, though I've encountered a number Zombies and Skeletons here, I haven't seen a single Flesh Golem... I thought.

"But if the Lich did such research, why didn't he use it?" I asked. "It sounds pretty strong."

"Clearly, it was because he couldn't control it," said Hugo. "The problem with the grudge power plan was that it involved absorbing the grudge from the surroundings. That was the prime obstruction to any success it could've had."

Hugo momentarily stopped talking and made the child on his back sit on his shoulders instead. Then, with his hands free, he raised up both of his index fingers.

"When a Necromancer uses grudge to power a Living Armor or a Flesh Golem, he normally uses a single person's grudge or soul for a single unit."

He then raised all of his fingers on only his right hand, indicating either "five" or just "many."

"However, grudge power absorbs all the surrounding grudge," he said. "And it doesn't matter how many and varied the source creatures are."

That was enough for me to understand the problem.

"So the individual grudges start fighting for the lead, and that makes the thing impossible to control, right?" I asked.

"Right," he nodded. "At least, that's what happened with the experimental machines our clan created. Our people then tried using both magic techniques and programming to ensure control, but apparently, their efforts were in vain."

Grudge-powered creatures seemed comparable to action game characters that were being controlled by tens of people fighting for the controller. There was no way they'd act properly.

"In the end, they went on rampages and began acting based on the consensus of the grudges," he went on.

"Consensus?" I raised an eyebrow.

"It always boiled down to the expansion of the grudge. They'd begin attacking either undead or other grudge power machines and attempt to merge with them. Then they'd react to the grudge — and negative emotions in general — of the living, and attack them instead. They'd continue rampaging like that until they broke."

...*Man, that sounds bad,* I thought.

"And so, the project was a failure," Hugo continued. "It was made clear that, while the grudge of many could be gathered and used for offense with skills such as Deadly Mixer, unifying and controlling it was a fool's errand."

"I see." I nodded.

As we talked, we finished going up the stairs and finally returned to the surface.

"...Huh?" I said.

A moment later, Nemesis, I, Cyco, Hugo and even the children... all shook with dread.

I could feel weak vibrations below me and heard voices coming from the outside — though it was arguable whether the term "voices" was appropriate. It was more like a choir of the macabre. Weeping, crying, sobbing, bellowing and just about any other possible sound representing negative emotion. That was more than enough for me to grasp that something alarmingly abnormal was happening outside.

"…Hey, Hugo." Urged by the bad feeling I had — or, rather, the very certain chills going down my spine — I spoke up.

"Yes?" he replied.

"If grudge power isn't controllable… what would happen if you used it regardless?"

"Heh, that's obvious," he said.

Beyond the gates leading outside, within the light of the sun sinking to the horizon, I saw the shadow of something massive.

"The uncontrolled grudge-powered thing would start absorbing the surrounding grudge, converting it into power, reacting to negative emotions, killing the source if it's alive, and once again absorbing the residual grudge," Hugo said.

I heard a loud roar and felt the ground under my feet vibrate as the massive *thing* shuddered and shifted.

"It would repeat that ad infinitum… and thus you'd have a rampaging monster equipped with a semi-permanent engine."

The beast outside the fortress came into sight. It looked like it came straight out of hell.

The first thing I saw were its repulsive legs, clearly made from human corpses. Then, as it moved nearer, I became certain of what it was.

The creature with the words "Revenant Ox-Horse, Gouz-Maise" above its head was a gigantic undead that seemed more abnormal

197

the more I looked at it. It had the head of an ox, the silhouette of a horse-man, and dead, familiar faces mixed in with the parts forming it. And it had a naming pattern used only by Unique Boss Monsters.

The visages of the dead were voicing words or merely sounds that were thick with negative emotion.

They were the Gouz-Maise Gang members that Hugo had killed. I could even see the faces of those we'd encountered back in Gideon.

...That was enough for me to conclude that it was made of the corpses of the gang.

"I see," said Hugo slowly. "It looks about the same as the predicted result."

Hugo took the documents out of his inventory and began looking through them. Sure enough, there was a picture of an ox-headed horse-man with countless dead faces on it.

"So he prepared for his own death by making a plan to create that thing by sacrificing everyone in the Gouz-Maise Gang," I said.

"Or perhaps he merely planned to use the surrounding corpses, and it just so happened that the ones around him were those of the bandits," added Hugo. "The ox-head, however, was a guaranteed ingredient."

Well, he's certainly following the plan, I thought.

"F f G g S s s F f f S s D d d W w S s S D d s S D d e E W w D A s s S a A A a a A a A———! !"

Gouz-Maise was passionately smashing something to pieces, letting out a roar no sane mind could comprehend.

Exposed to that noise, and such violence, the children started to scream in fear. Cyco embraced them to make them feel safe and gently tried to calm them down.

"Is that your…?" I began.

I noticed that the thing Gouz-Maise was breaking was the Magingear used by Hugo. Even though it no longer had a hint of its original shape, the monster didn't stop attacking it. Since it was running solely on the power of countless grudges, it was currently on a warpath. Due to that, I'd have expected it to spread its violence with no rhyme or reason, but it seemed to focus solely on the Magingear.

Are most of the ones that became the "ingredients" of that thing actually acting united due to their collective grudge towards Hugo and the robot? I thought.

"I'm the one who killed most of them, after all," he said. "It's only natural for my Marshall II to become its target."

So, even in that state, they haven't forgotten their resentments from when they were alive… Wait, no. It's more like that resentment is all that they are.

"Heh." Hugo grinned. "I feel like I'm looking at Rodin's Gates of Hell."

"Ironic of you to say that, Hugo," said Cyco.

The Gates of Hell, huh? I thought. *Yeah, watching this gathering of dead sinners is much like looking at that sculpture. And on the note of Rodin's sculptures, it's high time I stopped being The Thinker and actually did something about that abomination.*

"Well, Master?" spoke Nemesis. "Do we defeat it?"

"I'd love to if I can, but…" I could feel it in my bones. That thing was stronger than even Gardranda. Hell, I was certain that ten out of ten fights between Gouz-Maise and Gardranda would end in Gardranda's defeat.

"Man, creating UBMs is just unfair," I mumbled.

"Normally, it'd be completely impossible," said Hugo. "I know a person who can do something similar — with a higher standard, too — and even he has yet to create a single UBM. In fact, if it were possible to mass-produce UBMs, someone would be making them nonstop. After all, defeating them gets you special rewards."

So they could constantly create items such as my Miasmaflame Bracers, huh? I thought.

"That 'Revenant Ox-Horse, Gouz-Maise,'" he continued, "is the result of several unfortunate superimposed coincidences."

"Accidents?" I raised an eyebrow.

"First of all, this place is bad," he said. "It's an abandoned fortress on an ancient battlefield. There are tons of corpses filled with grudge right under our feet."

He pointed at the ground, then at himself.

"Second, I killed most of the gang. Due to that, the surroundings became thick with the grudge of vile scoundrels and got covered in fresh corpses. Corpses of people from a single group, even. There was even the Strong Gladiator Gouz — a real tough guy."

Next, he pointed at me.

"Third, you cornered Maise and pushed him into using the Crystal of Resentment — a concentrated gathering of grudge — as a medium to release a Deadly Mixer. Though you survived it, the dense grudge that didn't get used with the skill was released into the air. And let's not forget the Lich's own grudge after you killed him."

Finally, he pointed at Gouz-Maise.

"Lastly, someone activated the grudge-powered undead creation spell that was mentioned in the papers — Undead Grudge Construction. It used the surrounding grudge and corpses to form a grudge-powered Flesh Golem. However, due to the conditions being far too good, the resulting undead greatly surpassed its original specifications and — because of how abnormal and otherworldly it was — reached the realm of UBMs. With a slight change of perspective, it's safe to say that this creature is the child born from you, me, and the Lich."

"Well, that sure sucks," I said. "So, what now?"

"We simply lack the power to face it," replied Hugo. "It's far too strong an enemy for just two high-rank Masters and their low-rank Embryos. Not only that, but — as things are — it's highly incompatible with Cyco's power, and… well, just look at my weapon."

After shifting his gaze at the Magingear — which was reduced to a pile of scrap with pieces so small they could each be held in hand — Hugo heaved a long sigh.

I could still use Vengeance is Mine in the same way I'd used it against Gardranda, but it would be far more complicated in this case. Since the battle with the demon, I had gotten some levels, equipped the Miasmaflame Bracers, learned Purifying Silverlight, and become stronger overall.

However, the difference between Gardranda and *that thing* was just far too great. Its size alone was at least four times greater. Its height was about the same as that of an eight-story building. And naturally, its stats were much higher. I wasn't confident that I could survive until I charged up the damage needed to kill it. I also had only one more Counter Absorption use.

There's little doubt that I'd die if I fought it, I thought.

"True," agreed Nemesis. "…Hm?"

What's wrong? I asked.

"I just felt something strange… but it instantly went away. Was I just imagining it?"

"Ray," Hugo addressed me. "For now, our priority should be taking the children — including the ones in the carriages — and leaving this place as quickly as possible."

He pointed at the two carriages with the newly-kidnapped children inside them. Unlike the one at the front — which Hugo had destroyed with his preemptive attack — those two were in fine shape.

It was good thing that Gouz-Maise was too busy destroying the Magingear to do anything to harm the children. I could only assume that it was because they were sleeping, and thus weren't releasing any negative emotions that could've attracted it. Whatever the case, it was good that they were okay.

"Yeah, the carriages look ready to go at any time," I said. Both of them were already linked to horses.

Why didn't it attack the horses, though? I thought. *Does it only react to people?*

"Thankfully, both Cyco and I have the Piloting skill," said Hugo. "It works with carriages, too, to a certain extent, so we can both handle one carriage each."

"What about after we escape, though?" I asked. "Just leaving it there to do its thing doesn't seem like a good idea."

"We'll go to the Adventurer's Guild and tell them everything about it," answered Hugo. "It's a UBM, after all. There will be lots of Masters who'll go after it to get the special reward. Though, since I'm with Dryfe, you'll have to be the one to tell them about it."

"All right," I nodded. "Now, let's find the right timing to get to the carriages and… Ah!"

As we were about to act out the plan we'd set up, the situation suddenly changed.

We had been too unobservant…

…and we had failed to consider a certain scenario.

"Mommyyy! Daddyyy!"

It was the scenario in which the children in the carriages woke up and walked out of them.

"G g H h u U s S s D d S s s D c C a A a a S s s W w g G b b B a A S A a A A ! !"

Releasing a scream that nature surely didn't intend, Gouz-Maise turned around. Its gaze became fixed on the crying children, all exuding the negative emotion we knew as "fear."

"g G o O l l L f f F f A a S s s A a a A a A a a A ! !"

It was hard to tell whether the action was caused by the consensus of all the grudges, or the *eating habits* one of them had had while it was alive. However, Gouz-Maise's intentions were clear the moment it began running towards the children. Its right arm was extended towards them, saliva was pooling from its mouth.

"Damn it!" Before I could even think things through, I'd jumped out through the gate, and aimed my left bracer at the abomination. "Purgatorial Flames — full power!"

The Miasmaflame Bracer began violently draining my MP and converting it into fire. Though it was less intense than the deadly flame once used by the Great Miasmic Hobgoblin, Gardranda, the blaze I launched could easily reduce a hundred standard undead to ash, and it went straight for the arm that Gouz-Maise was extending towards the children.

"Y e E g a a A a x X A x S s A a a A f F f a a A a a A a ? !"

The way it screamed and swung its arm around was enough reason to believe that — despite being reduced to an amalgam of corpses — Gouz-Maise still felt pain.

"Take this! Gahh!!" Making use of the opportunity, I closed in on it and swung Nemesis — blessed with the Silverlight — at its front left leg.

The undead-killing shine split apart the dead faces of the gang and severely damaged both flesh and bone.

Though the leg was too thick for my attack to sever it, it was enough to make the abomination lose its balance.

"Cutting it feels awful!" Nemesis squealed in disgust.

Gouz-Maise dropped to the ground and made it shake like a demolished building would. As I'd somewhat intended, the monster's body landed in the direction opposite to the carriages.

"Hugo!" I shouted. "I'll divert its attention! Leave this to us and get out of here!"

"Ray, but you…!"

I knew what he wanted to say. If the carriages left, I wouldn't be able to run away from Gouz-Maise. Though I had Silver, I couldn't ride him, and my legs weren't fast enough to let me outrun the abomination. My death penalty would be guaranteed, and I'd end up missing the time we'd decided on with Marie.

However…

"There's no other option!" I shouted again. "Hurry up and get the children out of here!"

I brandished Nemesis, kept her blessed with the Silverlight, closed in on Gouz-Maise's head — which was near the ground due to it falling over — and swung at its eyes. Though my prime objective was to buy time for Hugo and the children, I still wanted to try my best to survive… and perhaps even win.

"GEeeHAaaAuAassSaAgGAa!!"

As liquid rot oozed out of its eye sockets, Gouz-Maise began to writhe. Due to its great size, the vibrations caused by that action were like a minor calamity.

"This thing's body is unexpectedly fragile," I commented.

"It's a gathering of cadavers, after all. It's only natural for it to not be particularly tough," said Nemesis. "However..."

"...Yeah, I expected it to have such tricks up its sleeve."

Once the fire on its arm faded, new rotten flesh popped up from under the carbonized skin. The leg, too, fixed itself while releasing some filthy fluids. The eyes I'd split fell out of their sockets and were replaced by new ones.

"It has Automatic Restoration," said Nemesis.

But undead hit by Silverlight are supposed to have wounds that will not heal, I thought. *How can it restore itself from that?*

"I believe the grudge power is being used to sustain and mend its large corpus," said Nemesis.

And that allows it to come back from such great damage in mere seconds? Is it unkillable or something?

"Well, it's already dead," said Nemesis.

"Not the time for such jokes!"

Still on the ground, the UBM swung its left arm at me, which I avoided by jumping backwards.

The swing seemed rather clumsy — probably due to its eyesight not being back yet — but it was still aimed at my direction.

Backing away from the carriages, I focused on evading its attacks.

"What now?" asked Nemesis. "We've opened hostilities on the fiend, but we don't really have anything that would be effective against it."

"The regeneration is too fast for most of our attacks to have any meaning," I said. "If there's something we can do, it's…"

…the same thing we'd done against Gardranda — a well-charged Vengeance aimed at its weak spot.

"Though the charging process would be really difficult here," I muttered. The fiend's defense was much lower than I'd expected, but the way it was rampaging was more than enough to show just how powerful it was. One or two good hits would kill me.

"It would've been grand to have a full stock of Counter Absorptions, but… oh, there's that strange feeling again," said Nemesis.

"What?" I asked.

"It's the same feeling as before," she said. "It has something to do with my accumulated damage counter and… Oh, it's gone again. What am I supposed to make of this?"

"Gouz-Maise might be up to something," I said. "Be on your guard."

"No need to tell me that."

As I talked with Nemesis, I looked at the carriages at the edge of my vision. Hugo and Cyco were sitting on separate carriages and were about to drive off.

I was about to make sure that Gouz-Maise didn't attack them by cutting its leg again but… the abomination wasn't moving at all. Instead, it simply used its freshly-healed eyes to stare directly at me.

"GgiiINnnNNnAsSaaAsSssaaSaAaAaSAd DWwDwWdDaAQqAq!!"

Acknowledging my form made it feel or remember something that caused it to release a furious roar.

"...Oh, I see," I said. A few minutes ago, the grudge of those who had become materials for Gouz-Maise had caused it to go on a rage and vehemently attack Hugo's Magingear. However, this monster had been created by the Lich himself, whose grudge was in it, as well. Thus, its primary target was...

"...me, of course!" I yelled.

Gouz-Maise raised its front legs and reared like a horse. Then, with great speed, it threw its pillar-like front legs towards me and the ground beneath.

I quickly evaded it, but the attack was powerful enough to pulverize the ground and sink it slightly. Not missing the opportunity, I closed in to attack a leg again, but unlike before, it nimbly kicked me away.

"GUH!" I blocked it with the broad side of my greatsword, yet I still got blown away about six meters back.

"...Well, looks like someone got in the mood," I said.

Unlike before, when it had simply been rampaging, Gouz-Maise was now moving with the intention to kill me. Apparently, seeing me had caused it to get serious.

"How troublesome," I mumbled.

"However, I now see a glimmer of hope for us," said Nemesis.

"What? How?"

I checked on the carriages at the edge of my vision. They were moving away from here.

Well, that's one success, I thought.

"You know how I told you about my accumulated damage counter?" asked Nemesis.

"Yeah," I nodded.

"The damage we received just now made me understand what was causing it. It was happening because it had already given us a great... no, the *greatest* amount of damage we've ever accumulated against a single creature."

"What?" I asked.

The greatest amount? But we only just started fighting it.

"Remember Deadly Mixer?" she said. "The skill the Lich used before you killed him? We absorbed its damage with Counter Absorption, but we ended up not having to use Vengeance. It's still there."

"Wait, that doesn't make sense," I said. "The Lich and Gouz-Maise are separate... Oh."

I suddenly understood. Lich Maise and Revenant Ox-Horse, Gouz-Maise were different... but not completely separate.

"The Lich's grudge is in there, after all," Nemesis continued. "Thus, the accumulated damage is still valid. However, it seems to come and go at random. Vengeance will probably only be effective when his grudge is the dominant one."

One Gouz-Maise body. Tens of grudges controlling it. My chance at defeating it existed only when it was being possessed by the grudge of the Lich.

"I see how it is," I nodded. All I had to do now was find the core and hit it with Vengeance is Mine while Maise was the one in charge. Though still challenging, defeating the abomination was no longer a fool's errand.

So...

"It's possible for us to win against this undead," said Nemesis.

"Good enough for me." I readied myself.

…There was only one thing left for me to do.

It was exactly the same thing I'd done when I'd fought the Demi-Dragon Worm and the Great Miasmic Hobgoblin, Gardranda. I simply had to give my all to that possibility.

"GEerRrrRuuUUAaASzDdSsAaaAAa!!"

As the fiend bellowed out the sound of its grudge, the faces and mouths covering its body began to whisper, oozing pus and blood as they did so.

"You won't escape!"

"You're dead!"

"Join us!"

"Kill them all!"

"Destroy!"

"Eat!"

"Ravage!"

Those were the kinds of things they were saying.

Even after they'd become a giant abomination, these men were thinking the exact same things they had when they were alive. Thus…

"Revenant Ox-Horse, Gouz-Maise!" Nemesis shouted. "You beasts who have inflicted great suffering upon countless younglings, taken many lives and are still endangering the living…"

I pointed my greatsword towards it. "We refuse to let you kill anyone ever again!"

I looked straight up into its eyes, and became one with Nemesis as we both proclaimed:

"You will fall by our hand!"

Now, about ten minutes since it had begun, our battle against the Revenant Ox-Horse, Gouz-Maise reached peak intensity. I was searching for its core, while the abomination tried to crush me beneath its feet. The battle would end the moment either of us were successful.

Both of us had attack potential that surpassed the opponent's HP. Gouz-Maise's offensive ability was truly overwhelming. Unlike Maise, it didn't use undead or cast magic debuff skills, but its physical prowess was incomparable to that of the Lich.

A single punch or kick could put me on the verge of death. I had only one use of my fatal attack. The conditions weren't in my favor.

"Hhah!!"

To both divert the abomination's attention and make it lose its balance, I swung Nemesis — blessed with the Silverlight — towards its leg.

"GDdESsaaAaAASsAaAa!!"

As the thing howled in pain, I jumped backwards.

A moment after I distanced myself from it, Gouz-Maise swept its leg through the place where I was standing. By that time, the wound had already healed.

I'd been repeating the same attack for a while now. I probably looked stupid, but through such repetition, people could notice things they didn't before.

"I was wondering why this undead thing could heal from wounds left by Silverlight... and I've finally figured it out," I announced.

I could see small bits of flesh sticking to the area around its injuries. At first glance, they looked like pieces I'd chopped off with my attacks. However, they were actually flesh that had it cut off *by itself.*

"It removes the flesh around the injury and then restores itself by multiplying its cells."

To undead like Gouz-Maise, wounds from weapons enchanted with Silverlight were unmendable. Thus, the abomination simply killed the cells surrounding the wound, disconnected the wound from itself, and effectively turned the Silverlight injury into normal damage. Since the corpses used in its creation were fresh, the cells were still alive, so making them multiply for healing purposes wasn't a hard task. That was the reasoning behind the trick.

The restoration was probably done by using the energy of the same grudge driving it. Also, Gouz-Maise was protecting the living cells from dying. This trick was impossible for Skeletons — since they were nothing but bone — and Zombies — since most of their cells were dead.

But man, grudge energy sure is versatile, I thought. *I can see why the Imperium wanted to utilize it.*

"So the cells are alive..." said Nemesis. "Though that comes with the demerit of pain sensitivity, which is unusual for undead."

"Seems like it," I nodded.

I'd gained some experience fighting undead during the night I'd spent in the Tomb Labyrinth. Not a single Skeleton or Zombie I'd fought there seemed to care about any damage they'd received. Thus, it was fair to assume that sensitivity to pain was a feature unique to Gouz-Maise.

"Or perhaps the Lich deliberately left the pain sensitivity in to make any damage caused to it increase its grudge," mused Nemesis.

"I see," I said. "So it could be less of a demerit and more like a proper part of the equatio—"

Before I could finish my sentence, I had to jump to the side. A moment later, the abomination's hoof landed right where I'd been standing.

While evading it, I swung my greatsword and cut into the hoof. The injury that caused was weaker than the previous ones, but if Gouz-Maise wanted to detach it and restore itself, it would surely lose its balance.

"Purgatorial Flames!" I complemented that wound with a stream of fire from my left Miasmaflame Gauntlet.

"H h o o O S s S D d A A S s a a A A a A h h ! ! "

It staggered and fell over, making the ground shake.

"GAH!!" I screamed, using the opportunity to get to its side. I changed Nemesis into The Flag Halberd and forced her into the area where the heart should've been. The Silverlight burned and melted both the faces on the surface and the rotten flesh under them before reaching the heart behind its ribcage.

"G E E E E A A A A A A E E e e E E e e A A a a A A a a E e e E e A A A A A ! ! "

Though the scream the monster released as it writhed violently was of a higher pitch than the previous ones, it didn't show any signs of becoming weaker.

Its flesh and skin fixed themselves the moment I pulled Nemesis out. That applied to the heart, as well.

"Doesn't seem like the core is in the heart!" I shouted.

"Then it must be the head!" said Nemesis.

Reason suggested that cores had to be put in either the heart area, the head area, or in the stomach area, as it had been with

Gardranda. Due to other parts of the body being used in combat, no one in their right mind would put such a weak spot in the limbs.

After all, that would be the equivalent of punching people with your own innards, I thought.

"Or hitting them with your testicles!" added Nemesis.

I'm not fond of that example in any way whatsoever.

"Now, it's fine if it's in the head," I said. "But things would get a bit troublesome if it's in the stomach."

Once you included the horse part, the monster's stomach was pretty damn large. If the core was in there, searching for and destroying it would be extremely difficult. If it was doable, I wanted to use Vengeance is Mine while directly touching the core.

"Why?" asked Nemesis. "With the current amount of accumulated damage, it'll be possible to destroy a considerably large part of its body."

Well, it was true that the hit I'd landed on Gardranda's head had also destroyed its chest, but...

"It's different this time," I said. "With this self-amputation thing Gouz-Maise has going on, there's a chance that it could negate the damage from Vengeance."

I didn't know what would happen if I landed Vengeance on the general area of the core and it suddenly detached the part that I'd hit. However, I had a feeling that the spread of the damage wouldn't go beyond the detached part.

That assumption was based on my experience as one who'd used Vengeance is Mine many times before. No matter how great the damage I'd give back to my enemies, the skill never seemed to have a noticeable effect on the surroundings. Vengeance merely doubled the damage I received from hostiles and gave it back to them — it didn't do any physical damage on its own. So, if the abomination could detach the part of the body I hit, there was a chance that the damage — no matter how great — wouldn't reach the core. I couldn't risk having my one chance go to waste like that.

"The best move right now is hitting the undetachable core and *then* using the skill," I said. "Now, let's try the skull!"

"Understood!" said Nemesis. "First, we have to make it fall to the ground again!"

Gouz-Maise was already standing tall, and the wounds we'd given it were gone without a trace.

We'll get it to the ground, hit its head, see how it reacts and... Huh?

"G h u o o h..."

For some reason, it had completely stopped moving. The creature had shifted its gaze away from me and was staring somewhere far into the distance.

"Master," Nemesis said.

"What is it, Nemesis?" I asked.

"The accumulated damage counter has disappeared."

"Wait, you don't mean that..."

The moment I understood what she meant by that, Gouz-Maise had already begun moving.

"G l i i o o U u J j j a a a A a A ! !"

Unlike before, it now completely ignored me and started to run to where Hugo and Cyco had taken the carriages. Nemesis' words and the abomination's actions led me to the one reasonable conclusion.

"Damn it!"

The dominant grudge has changed! I thought, panic setting in. I didn't know if it happened because of the repeated restoration making the total grudge level drop or because I'd destroyed the heart once. However, it was obvious that the body was now being controlled by a grudge that didn't belong to the Lich.

From the fact that it was going after Hugo, it was safe to assume that it was someone he'd killed. Or perhaps it was only going after the children so it could kill them and stock up on more resentment.

"What now?!" screamed Nemesis.

"We'll do what we have to!" I yelled back.

To defeat Gouz-Maise, I had to find a means to make the Lich's grudge the dominant one again. And I happened to have a plan for that.

"Where is it…?" I asked while looking at the ground. "Found it."

I picked up a certain item and put it into my pocket rather than the inventory. With that, I was prepared. The only problem now was catching up to the monster. I needed something that could let me move fast enough to catch up to that semi-equestrian body.

I don't have the time to hesitate about this, I thought.

"Silver!"

My mount instantly answered my call and ran over to my side.

"…You're doing *that* again?" asked Nemesis.

"Not like I have any other options," I replied. "Though it should be a bit better than before."

I grabbed a piece of detached Magingear armor that was lying on the ground and put it under my feet. Then I grabbed hold of Silver's reins…

"Away!"

…and ordered him to move.

He soon began speeding through the road. Holding on to his reins, I was trailing right beside him while using the armor plate to slide on the ground.

Fortunately, the path we were following was a simple dirt road with no tree-like flora on it. It was good enough for the armor plate to slide on relatively smoothly. Though it was only slightly better than having my feet get dragged on the ground, I didn't mind it. After all, I was certain that I could catch up to Gouz-Maise this way.

"Don't forget to heal when necessary," said Nemesis.

"I know." I cast First Heal on myself.

Water skiing: land edition was a little bit too hard on my legs. If I didn't heal, the damage to my feet by the time I arrived would be severe enough to render me unable to walk.

After a few minutes of such sliding…

"I see it!" shouted Nemesis.

"Me too!"

…we found the giant creature. Its base form was that of a horseman, but since Maise — the only one there who knew how to move such a body — wasn't the one in charge, it wasn't running as fast as it could. Silver's speed was more than enough for us to catch up to it.

"But man, this is bad," I said. "I can see Hugo's group less than a hundred meters away from it."

"At this rate, it will…" Nemesis cut her words short. "Can't you use the Miasmaflame Bracers' flamethrower?!"

"No."

I couldn't launch Purgatorial Flames because Silver's movement speed was greater than the projectile speed of the fire. Not only would it not reach Gouz-Maise, it'd end up burning *us*.

However, the creature was going to reach the carriages before we caught up with it.

"Hey, wait," I said. "I still have some of those, don't I?"

As I held the reins with my right hand, I used my left to reach into my inventory and take something out.

"Those are…!" Nemesis seemed surprised.

"Guess leaving some of these unused worked in our favor!" I cried.

And so, I threw the items — the leftover White Lance Gems I'd used against Spirits while leveling in the Tomb Labyrinth — towards the abomination. Mid-air, the Gems changed into spears of light and went straight towards the back right leg of Gouz-Maise.

These Gems were basically the market's substitutes for offensive magic. Though the spell inside was a skill from low-rank jobs, it was purely anti-undead. Its effects were evident the moment the White Lances hit Gouz-Maise's leg as it ran. A fist-sized hole opened up in its flesh, causing it to completely lose its balance and fall to the ground.

"Go!" I shouted.

Silver closed the distance between us and the abomination. I brandished Nemesis in my left hand, enchanted her with Silverlight, and had Silver go parallel to the creature.

Syncing my attack with my horse's running, I sunk the blade into Gouz-Maise's body. Breaking through the many faces on its skin, my silver sword cut through its back.

First, it was the horse-like back, then the part linking the horse and human bodies, then the back of the human-like body. I evenly split the spinal cord.

"G a E i I r u U r R u u O u u U e e E A a a E K e e a A A ! !"

Releasing a scream from all the mouths it had, the abomination writhed and tried to crush us, but Silver quickly fixed the distance between us and went out of its reach.

"It's not over yet!" I roared.

My blade went through its back, cervical vertebrae, skull, and finally reached the brain.

"GhH!! DaSqQ! AaSz! wQaA?!"

It released cries of pain that were completely unlike any previous ones and quickly got up with an intense jump. That action made me release the reins, and I was thrown several meters away, dropping to the ground with a roll. The impact made me turn off the Silverlight. However, it was fully worth it.

"That reaction was...!" said Nemesis.

"Found it!" I shouted.

It had reacted to that damage in a completely different way than before. There was no room for doubt that the core was in its skull.

"This is where we'll end the battle," I said.

I took out the thing in my pocket and threw it upwards. It was a piece of a shattered crystal. Specifically — a piece of the Crystal of Resentment that the Lich had so treasured.

"HEEIYAAASAASAGAAAAAAA!"

Upon seeing the shard, Gouz-Maise released a roar that seemed somewhat unlike the others. I felt like it was thick with desolation, frustration, and regret.

"The accumulated damage counter is back!" shouted Nemesis. "He's the one controlling it!"

Just as planned.

"Let's bring it down to the ground!" I yelled.

"All right!"

I channeled the Silverlight again and used all of my STR, buffed by the Miasmaflame Bracers, to jump. The shock caused by me preparing for the jump made the ground under my right foot crack, but I paid it no heed. The jump covered more than ten meters worth of distance and put me right next to Gouz-Maise's legs.

"Ghh…!"

Going all-out took a toll on my muscles and brought them close to tearing, while my right leg turned somewhat numb.

Still, I'll end it here and now! I thought.

Using my left leg — the one I'd landed with — as the origin, I put the impact and speed of the jump into my greatsword and swung it at the abomination's front right leg.

"SPLIT APAAAAAART!"

With the sounds of a slash and Silverlight's light burning, the blade smoothly cut through its skin, flesh, and skeleton. Gouz-Maise's leg bone was completely cleaved open. The skin and flesh on the opposite side of the cut wasn't enough to let the leg function and made the creature lose its balance. Obviously, it instantly tried to detach the wound and fix it, but…

"Not happening! Haaaahh!!!" I followed up my attack with another slash aimed at the injury, causing its leg to break off completely. Without its support, Gouz-Maise lost all the balance it had left and fell to its right.

I used my left leg to jump away from there and then ran straight towards the place where its head was about to land.

The plan was simple — hit it with Vengeance is Mine.

"With this…" I screamed.

…it's done! I added silently. *Victory is ours! We've won!*

I suddenly had a feeling that we weren't the only ones to think that. As the distance between me and Gouz-Maise's head shortened, an inexplicable chill went down my spine, and not for the first time, either. It was much like the one I'd felt when I was about to launch my final attack on Gardranda.

My eyes met with the two eyes on its face... and the third eye on its forehead.

No. There was no such thing. That wasn't an eye.

The thing peeking out of its torn forehead was a gem-like stone that didn't reflect any light.

What is that? I thought.

But I knew exactly what it was. It was the abomination's core.

Why had it revealed it to us — the ones trying to destroy it?

"...!"

The answer to that came in the form of great gathering of energy that started to whirl around its forehead. It was reminiscent of something I'd already experienced today — the transformation of grudge into unbridled, overwhelming power.

The *Deadly Mixer*.

The magical destructive force the Lich had used for his last stand.

I'd been too careless. The fact that Gouz-Maise didn't manipulate undead or use magic debuff skills had made me believe that it couldn't use this, either. However, Hugo had said that Gouz-Maise operated by transforming grudge into energy. Thus, it was perfectly reasonable for it to be able to use Deadly Mixer, which worked on the same principle.

Still on the ground, the abomination fixed its aim on us as we closed in on its head. Just like myself, the thing was looking for a good opportunity to finish me off. Its grudge helped...

No — its grudge was the very reason why it was able to gather its shattered intelligence and devise a plan to end the life of the one it was compelled to kill.

"**D d E e A a A D d d L l L y y Y y y MmM i i l x x X e e e E E e r R r r R R r !**"

Due to Gouz-Maise being an amalgam of grudge, the sorcery that it released, which converted grudge into destructive power, was nearly instantaneous.

"Counter Absorption!" I screamed.

I hastily extended Nemesis and used the last Counter Absorption I had in stock. That was enough to block its Deadly Mixer. However, that didn't save me from being placed into checkmate.

After all, the distance between us had become short...

Short enough for its arms to reach me.

Guarding against the Deadly Mixer had rendered me unable to move. Gouz-Maise used the opportunity to swing its boulder-like fists at me. The next moment, my body was launched into the air... and my consciousness faded.

Maiden of Vengeance, Nemesis

Right after we used Counter Absorption to block Gouz-Maise's Deadly Mixer, its large fists hit Ray's body. Still holding me in my greatsword form, my Master was blasted to the side. Passing between the trees in the forest, he flew through the air like a leaf in the wind.

The scene was reminiscent of a truck accident from Ray's memory... and the time the Superior Killer had given him his first death penalty.

"Ray!" I called out to him, but he didn't answer.

He had already lost consciousness. And his unconscious body was heading straight for a tree.

"Ah!" I quickly went into my human form, held him from behind, and tightly closed my eyes. A moment later, I felt a strong impact and pain spread through my back. As the tree we hit shook, we both fell to the ground beneath.

"Khh... Ah..." The pain was still there after we hit the surface. The impact I'd felt when squeezed between the tree and Ray — who was considerably larger than me — seemed to have made my ribs crack. However, I was certain that it prevented Ray from feeling any of that pain. That was more than enough for me.

"Ray!" I called out to him, but he didn't show any signs of waking up.

Looking at his status, I saw that his HP was below 10% and that he had status effects such as Fainting and several Bone Fractures. Reaching into his inventory, I took out an HP recovery Potion and poured it over him. That healed some of his HP, but it didn't take care of a single one of his status effects. The wounds were simply too deep. Also, Potion-type consumables were more effective when ingested, and due to being unconscious, Ray couldn't drink any Potions I tried giving him.

"Forgive me!" I poured the content of the Potion into my mouth and pushed my lips against his. I then did it two more times. With that, I got Ray to swallow an entire bottle's worth of medicine.

It became effective almost instantly, healing about a third of his HP and fixing the lighter Bone Fractures. His HP stopped going down, as well.

Though Ray was still unconscious, it was clear that he was no longer on the verge of dying. However, I was unsure if I could look him in the eye after this.

"Now's not the time to think about that!" I cried desperately.

We were still in a particularly dire situation. I could hear tremors encroaching towards us, warning me that Gouz-Maise was getting closer. If the aberration saw Ray in this state, it would instantly kill him.

He would die a second time.

"I won't allow that."

I couldn't stomach the idea of Ray being killed by that *thing*.

"Ray," I said.

Still unconscious, my Master was lying near the tree we'd hit.

I gently caressed his cheek and turned away from him. "I will buy you some time."

I believe in you. The evening after we lost to the Superior Killer, we made a promise. Back then, we were both weak and could do nothing against him. Thus, we agreed to become stronger and emerge victorious. Now, we both fight as one. I know you will wake up soon. So I will buy you all the time you need... because that is what will lead us to victory.

"Here I go!" I transformed my right hand into a black blade. Though relatively small, it was about as strong a weapon as my sword form.

I shoved myself in front of Gouz-Maise before it could find Ray. "You're not getting past me, Gouz-Maise!"

"DHISSSSIIIIUAAAAAAA!!"

Every face on its body screamed. Each and every eye on its body swiveled and fixed on me.

The counter within me didn't react, which meant that it wasn't being controlled by the Lich's grudge. It had noticed me simply because I was a living creature.

I had to face it and keep it occupied long enough for Ray to wake up.

"Augh!" I used my right hand-blade to attack Gouz-Maise.

My strategy was the same as Ray's. I attacked it, was attacked back, and evaded.

Though Gouz-Maise was tough and powerful, it wasn't fast at all. Even I didn't have any problems dodging its attacks.

However, unlike when Ray had swung me, I didn't seem to be able to hurt it at all. Without Silverlight, the most I could do was give it the most meager of cuts.

My stats were far below Ray's. Not only that, but I was out of uses of the one skill I could do by myself — Counter Absorption.

Gouz-Maise, on the other hand, attacked me with nothing but blows that could kill me instantly. Unlike when I was a sword, a single direct hit would make my body shatter.

Though a single mistake could be fatal, I pressed on. If I gave up, the possibility of Ray waking up and us emerging victorious would become zero.

Neither Ray nor I could accept that. Thus, I fought to keep the possibility alive.

This feeling had been within me ever since I was born. I was certain that Ray had it, as well.

It was the one true thing that kept us tethered and connected.

Paladin Ray Starling, within a dream

I instantly understood that I was dreaming.

I still had the appearance of my *Infinite Dendrogram* avatar, but everything felt somewhat *hazy*, making me feel like I was in a lucid dream.

Despite that, however, I had no trouble processing my situation and the state of my surroundings. For example, I could clearly see a child — a young me, to be precise — running somewhere.

"Oh... I remember this," I said.

I could easily tell that this dream depicted the past. I even knew the time. It was the summer of 2035 — nearly ten years ago.

Obviously, *Infinite Dendrogram* hadn't been out yet, so my brother and I were playing different games.

Back then — when he was 16 — Shu had been all about retro games and martial arts. He'd gradually improved his fighting skills by frequenting a long-running dojo run by the family of our sister's friend, and he'd eventually become a considerably famous contestant through U-17 — a tournament for minors.

My days back then had consisted of playing retro games with him while looking forward to seeing his matches. On days when those happened, I'd tended to head to the venues they were held in while being all giddy about it.

Just like in this memory.

"Man, what *is* this?" I muttered.

My question was only natural. After all, I — as my avatar, Ray — was following my younger self. Not only that, but I had something unknown standing next to me. If I had to describe it with one word, it would've been "silhouette."

Yes — a humanoid silhouette was just floating in the middle of this normal-looking midsummer day. Its color was a mix of red and black, making it seem somewhat sinister. In my Ray form and still wearing all my armor, I was walking through this standard Japanese day with this silhouette by my side. The strangeness of this situation was another reason why I'd concluded that I was in a dream. Something this weird would only happen in a dream.

The silhouette was completely silent.

"How about you say something?" I spoke to it.

"R e p l a y," it said.

R-Replay?

"So this is your doing?" I asked.

Since the silhouette's voice was feminine, I momentarily assumed it was Nemesis, but I quickly got the feeling that it wasn't.

"I w a n t t o a s k."

Hey, I have several questions, too, I thought.

"T u r n s."

Turns…? So we'll take turns asking questions? I thought.

"Okay," I nodded.

And so, myself and this dark red silhouette that seemed to be able to read my mind had a little information exchange.

"W h e r e i s t h e b o y g o i n g?" asked the entity.

"The venue where my brother's having a tournament match," I answered. "This is when, uh…"

Of course, I knew exactly where I was heading, what was supposed to take place there… and what would actually happen.

"This is when he participated in Un-kra's U-17 tournament."

"U n - k r a?" The dark red entity questioningly tilted its head, but now it was my turn to ask a question.

"Tell me," I spoke up. "If this is a dream, then what's happening to me? I'm quite sure I was in the middle of fighting Gouz-Maise. Did I get the death penalty?"

That seemed unlikely, since it seemed like I was still in the game.

"A l i v e . . . F a i n t e d."

So I'm unconscious, huh? I thought. *...Wait, doesn't that mean that I'm open to getting hit by a finishing blow at any moment?*

"W h a t ' s U n - k r a?"

"A death match-type martial arts tournament with no weight limit, no style limit, no rules besides the use of weapons and threats, and no end without KOs and give ups — Unlimited Pankration. Also known as 'Un-kra.'"

It was a popular tournament that had begun — if I recalled correctly — in 2027. With it allowing karate, judo, boxing, kickboxing, sumo, wrestling, Muay Thai, capoeira, koryu, and countless other styles, it seemed like an event from some fighting manga. The level of violence earned it lots of criticism, but it continued to be popular regardless.

". . ." The silhouette looked somewhat excited.

Does it like martial arts? I asked myself. *Or death matches?*

"My turn to ask," I said. "How do you not know what Un-kra is if — as you said yourself — you're the one replaying this scene?"

Nemesis had had some of my memories since the moment she was created, so I found it weird that this entity didn't.

"O n l y . . . r e p l a y i n g . . . n e c e s s a r y . . . m e m o r i e s."

So it's replaying only the memories deemed necessary, huh? I thought. *But man, if it can scan my memories, yet isn't an Embryo... just what is it? I guess I could ask it directly...*

"W h a t w i l l h a p p e n n o w . . . ?"

I'd expect someone replaying the scene to know that much, I thought.

"Keep watching and you'll see in a few minutes," I said. "Now, my question: have we met before?"

"Y e s," it replied. "H e r e , w e a r e a l w a y s t o g e t h e r . . ."

"What...?" I said, baffled.

"Here," as in, within Infinite Dendrogram? *But the only person I'm always together with in this world is Nemesis.*

"B o y i s a l o n e , n o t d a n g e r o u s . . . ?" the silhouette asked while pointing at young me.

"The security system observing public roads was already there ten years ago, so no, I wasn't in danger of getting kidnapped or anything," I said.

I had trouble remembering when the security guard machines had become widespread. I had a feeling they'd already been there by the time I was born.

"S t i l l , a c h i l d b y h i m s e l f . . . ?"

"It might've been my summer holiday, but it was still a normal weekday for adults, so yeah. ...Wait, wasn't that a second question?"

"Ask t w i c e , t o o , Ray." Though its words were still monotonous, it was gradually getting better at talking.

"How can I regain consciousness?" I asked.

"Wake u p w h e n f i nished w a t ching."

"Finished watching what?" I asked.

"Your b i r t h."

M-My birth...?

"Watch why y o u beca m e t h e Ray y o u a r e."

"...I see," I said.

The reason why I turned out to be the way I am, huh? Seeing the events that are about to transpire will be more than enough to know that.

"Won't be long now." Saying that, I pointed at young me, who was walking before us.

He was already near the venue and only needed to walk through a pedestrian crossing to get to the entrance. As eight-year-old me waited for the traffic light to change, there was an even younger girl standing right next to him. She had a childish accessory in her hair, but due to the poor way she'd put it on, it flew off the moment a stronger gust of wind went by. It fell on the road.

The light was still green for traffic, and when the girl tried to go and take her accessory, she didn't notice the truck headed right for her. A few moments before it could hit her, the young me ran in, took her hand, and tried pulling her off the road. However, he was too slow and weak.

At eight years old, he was far too powerless to take her to safety before the truck hit them both. As a result, all young me did back then was simply increase the number of victims. And so, the truck was about to run over two children.

However, a moment later, a person who'd come over from the other side of the road took them both and jumped out of the way.

Normally, that person wouldn't have made it. In fact, normally that person wouldn't have made it even if he'd come over the moment the girl ran out to the road. However, the feat was perfectly possible for this person. Due to his astounding leg strength, he'd closed the distance in but a moment and swiftly taken the girl by the hand.

However, there was also me — who was nothing but a burden at this point. Due to me jumping out to the road, the person needed to take both of us. And though he was capable of jumping while holding two children, it — naturally — slowed him down.

I remembered it clearly. After a moment of being airborne, there was another impact. Then — while still being held — I rolled on the ground.

Even so, I didn't feel any pain. The person holding us did a great job protecting us. I could hear some people nearby start to scream. I, on the other hand, was at a loss for words.

That was only natural. After all — the one who'd saved us was my brother.

Knowing I was coming, he'd walked out to meet up with me. And it just so happened that he'd saw us in great peril and saved us. He'd paid a price for that — his right leg was hit by the truck. With how blue-black and swollen it was, you didn't need to be an expert to know that it was broken.

Shu was about to participate in the final match of the tournament. However, right before it happened, his leg got shattered...

...and it was all because of me trying to save the girl while being completely powerless to do so.

At a certain place in the City of Duels, Gideon

"Heyoo! Haven't seen you fur a while, Figgy."

"Oh? I know that voice, but not the face. A new costume, Shu?"

"You assume correctly. This is an MVP special reward called 'Hind Bear.'"

"…Another costume, I see."

"Yeah, it's another costume. Got a problem with that?"

"How many do you have by now?"

"Sorry, but that's not something I bear in mind. All I know is that I only have one that *isn't* a costume."

"…I see there's a bit of a bias."

"*Every* special reward besides the thing I got from Gloria is a costume! This makes bearly any sense!"

"It's quite unusual to be able to defeat so many UBMs, though."

"Sorry, but those words have bearly any weight when said by *you*, of all people."

"You're probably right. Oh, it just hit me… You've worn bear costumes since that time, right?"

"'That time,' as in…?"

"The time we met."

"Oh yeah, I was beary ursine back then, too. Though that one was store-bought."

"It was also the first time we fought UBMs, right?"

"Yeah. That takes me back."

"We sure had a hard time handling them."

"It happened when *Infinite Dendrogram* had only been out for only ten or so days, right? Our levels were still pretty low."

"Yep, that sounds about right."

"I'm still impressed that we were able to win... To be honest, looking back at it, it's actually beary weird that we did."

"But you didn't show any signs of giving up back then, right?"

"Ha ha ha! As if I would. Like I said back then: 'The possibility is always...'"

Paladin Ray Starling, within a dream of the past

On that summer day of 2035, my brother had gotten into an accident while protecting us. His life hadn't been in danger. However, his right leg — hit by the truck — had been seriously injured. The flesh was swollen, the blood vessels under the skin had burst, and the bone was broken. In a game, healing magic or items would've made short work of such a wound, but in reality, it was a grave injury that would need quite a while to be fixed.

It was bad enough for him to be hospitalized. And the tournament's final match was supposed to happen about an hour after he'd received it.

"Nothing t h a t cou l d be done?" asked the entity.

"Indeed," I nodded. "It was hopeless for him."

...If reason had its say, anyway, I thought.

I could see the passersby begin to surround us and make a stir. Some were panicking, others were calling ambulances, while some journalist-looking sorts who were focusing on my brother as a fighter in the final match called out to him with a "Mr. Mukudori!"

Standing next to my brother — who was lying on the ground — was young me and the girl, both crying. The girl was probably crying because of the fear of being involved in such an accident, while I was crying due to the fact that Shu had gotten injured because of me.

I could clearly remember the things I'd thought back then. It could be summed up as guilt about what I'd done to him mixed with begging someone to help him.

In response to all the sympathetic looks and my sentiment, my brother — still on the ground — looked at young me for a moment and...

"Owie!"

...jumped up after saying that in a tone one would use when accidentally hitting their head on a ceiling frame.

Everyone was dumbfounded.

The young me, the girl, and the passersby all looked at him with eyes open wide with shock. To add to that — even the silhouette right next to me seemed surprised.

"Well, darn... This sure looks broken," he said as he looked down on his broken right leg while standing on his healthy left. Yet again, his tone was unfitting, making him sound like he'd broken a piece of a plastic model rather than his limb. And no, it wasn't "better than it looked" — his leg was severely injured.

"That r e a ction is s t range." The silhouette made a comment.

"Well, it's him we're talking about, so yeah." I was used to seeing my brother act and talk like that by now. But the young me still hadn't had much exposure to his eccentricity at that point in time, so he was reasonably shocked.

"I-I just called an ambulance! It should be here soon! Please don't move too much!" one of the passersby told my brother.

However, in response, Shu said, "Eh? Oh... Well, thank you for the concern. But there's no need for that right now."

"'No need'?" a number of people simultaneously repeated his words in disbelief.

"I have a final match to participate in over at that building, so I'll go to the hospital after that's done," he said.

The moment he'd said that, I'd felt as though time had stopped.

It seemed like I and everyone else on the scene — except for my brother — was thinking exactly the same thing: *What is this guy saying?*

From its reaction, it was safe to assume that the silhouette shared the sentiment.

◇

The place of the dream changed, and we were now in Shu's waiting room.

Moments before this scene, this place had included doctor who'd given my brother some first aid and the master from his dojo who'd tagged along to see the fight, but they were no longer here. The only ones present now were me and Shu.

His right leg was covered in a compress and bandaged. But that was all. There was no cast or any kind of support on it. After all, Shu was about to go fight in the match. He'd refused casts and supports because they would've been counted as weaponry. The injury was bad enough to need an operation, and yet...

". . . H e w ill fight?" asked the entity.

"Yeah," I nodded.

Due to the lack of expression on the silhouette, it was hard to tell what it was thinking, but even I could tell that it was half amazed and half shocked. "No one s t o ps him?"

"In a normal martial arts tournament, the fight would've been called off due to doctor's orders, but this is Un-kra we're talking about."

Again, Un-kra allowed anything besides the use of weaponry and threats, and would only end with KOs and give-ups. It was actually strange that such a tournament could exist in this day and age.

"But it's b roken," the silhouette protested. "He ca n win? Doesn't nee d right l eg?"

"The koryu martial arts dojo my brother went to is based around blows, rather than throws and such," I answered. "Naturally, kicks are a crucial part of it, and proper leg control while punching is highly important, as well."

Now that I think about it, that style is ridiculously manga-like, I thought. *Seriously, during the demonstrations I saw, their kicks were breaking logs as thick as people's torsos. What was the name of that kick, again? All I can remember is that it sounded pretty cool.*

"Is h i s opponent w eak?" asked the entity.

"The opponent in the final match was Gregory Asimov Kaiser," I said. "He was nearly two meters tall and weighed over a hundred kilos, most of which was well-trained muscle. Being well-versed in blows, holds, throws, and locks, he was easily the strongest student participant at that time. He's now doing his best to be the top professional martial artist."

"Student... c h ild... child?"

"He was seventeen at that time, which is underage, so yeah." Also, even after ten years had passed, Gregory was still a well-known face in the end-of-year martial arts shows. Last New Year's Eve — when my brother had returned home for the occasion — I could recall us both watching TV and seeing Gregory still doing his thing.

"Brot her can' t wi n, n o?"

"He would've had little chance even if he was in top form, and yet he went in with a broken leg," I said. "It's only reasonable that people tried to stop him."

Not like he listened, I thought. *Now that I think about it, the master from his dojo was one of the few who didn't try to make him reconsider.*

"Shu, don't! If you fight someone so strong with *that* wound, you'll die!" The young me was still trying to get him to withdraw from the match.

That was only natural. After all, when Shu had gotten injured because of me, I'd been overwhelmed by great fear. And yet, despite his state, he was about to go on and do something reckless, if not downright crazy. My fear back then hadn't allowed me to stay silent and let him do it.

"Well, I guess doing the Kodachi with my leg like this isn't the best idea," said Shu, completely nonchalant.

Oh, yeah, I thought. *That's what the kick from his school is called.*

"Kodachi," the wood-splitter or "battle ax," was a frontwards roundhouse kick aimed at the opponent's head. My brother was particularly good at it. The kick which — as the name implied — was strong enough to split wood and seemed capable of doing the same to people's heads was feared as much as Gregory.

However, with his right leg broken, my brother couldn't do it anymore. He couldn't do it with his left leg, either, since he would've had to use his right as the pivot leg. Shu was going to have to fight without his ultimate kick.

That meant only one thing — he had no chance of winning.

He'd gotten the wound because of me. And since it was going to be the reason for his defeat — or perhaps even death — I couldn't stop blaming myself. Thus, I was trying to stop him.

However, Shu showed no sign of changing his mind. He was always like that. Though facetious and eccentric, my brother wasn't one to easily let go of something he'd resolved to do.

Once the young me came to understand that trying to convince him was useless, he bowed his head in sadness.

"I shouldn't have jumped out to the road..." he muttered to himself.

"Hmm." Hearing that, Shu thought about something, leaned over to the young me, placed his hands on his shoulders, and looked him in the eyes. "Honestly, Reiji... I think you would've regretted it more if you *hadn't* tried to save her."

"B-But you're the one who actually saved her!" the young me protested. "I couldn't do it by myself! All I did was get you hurt!" The young me wept about his powerlessness. All he felt was regret, grief, and anger at himself.

"You're right. I got hurt." Shu agreed with me. "But you know, it's entirely possible that I wouldn't have saved her if you hadn't tried it."

"Eh?" That surprised the young me.

"Because you tried to save the girl, I — without thinking — jumped out to save both of you," he explained. "In the end, she was saved because of *your* choice."

That might've been the truth, or just a lie to make me feel better. However, there was sincerity in his eyes.

"That's good enough, Reiji," he said. "There's no need to regret the act of choosing something. After all, it's the ultimate premise to grabbing hold of the possibility leading to the future you desire."

He added a lot of emphasis to the words that followed.

"After choosing something, all that matters is whether you can see it or not and grab hold of it or not."

"Grab hold of it or not?" the young me asked.

"Yeah. The possibility is always…"

These words of his…

"The possibility is always there — *with your will.* No matter how small, no matter behind how many zeros beyond the radix point it lies — it *always* exists. The only time the possibility isn't there is when you've given up on grabbing hold of the future you desire. As long as you don't give up and keep making choices towards the future you want to see, the possibility won't disappear, even if it's far beyond the radix point."

These words of his were still etched onto my very core.

"That's why your choice to save the girl back there wasn't a mistake," he added.

"Shu…" the young me said.

He gave the young me an intrepid smile and stood up. "Today's the perfect chance, so I'll show you the ropes. You'll soon see what it means to give your all to grab hold of the possibility."

With those words as his last, Shu left the waiting room and used his crutches to make his way to where the match would take place.

That was when the dream portraying my memories reached its end. The venue we were in vanished, leaving only an empty dreamscape vaguely reminiscent of a pale haze.

The young me and my brother were nowhere in sight, meaning that the only ones here now were me, as Ray, and the silhouette.

"Is it o v er?" asked the entity.

"Well, the match was supposed to happen right after this," I replied.

Though, if the dream's objective was to display my roots, it makes sense for it to end with the exchange between me and Shu, I thought.

"Can I ask a n o ther thi n g?"

"Sure." I knew exactly what it was gonna ask.

"Di d h e win?"

"He did."

Indeed — Shu had gone into the final match against Gregory and actually emerged victorious.

"H o w?" the silhouette asked.

Man, I really don't wanna say it, I thought. *Though I don't want to keep the silhouette in suspense, either, so I guess I will.*

The news about my brother's right leg being rendered useless had already spread among the people in the venue. Even the spectators around my seat had been talking about it. Also, the way Shu had gone towards the ring — crutches and all — had made him look extremely pitiful. While he was climbing into the ring, he hadn't let his right leg touch the floor beneath him. Having to use his left one alone had given him a really hard time and gotten people to understand just how bad of an injury it was.

For some reason, the people already knew that it was caused by an accident he'd gotten into while saving children, making him get lots of sympathetic glances. Some martial artists were praising him for not withdrawing from the match after getting such a grave wound, calling him "a true fighter."

His opponent, Gregory, shared the sentiment. "It's a shame I don't get to fight you at your best," he said. "Though I'm sure that one day we'll get to go all-out on each other."

Though he looked menacing, Gregory was actually quite a gentle person.

"I'm sure we will," replied my brother in a rather cheerful manner.

There was a difference in height. In weight class. And a critical problem with the state of one contestant. The outcome was clear. What was about to happen was nothing but a ritual-like event meant only to preserve my brother's pride and honor as a martial artist.

That was what everyone present thought.

Thus, the gong sounded… and Shu launched from his right leg, performed Kodachi, smacked Gregory across the jaw, and knocked him unconscious.

The match had ended there.

The fifth Unlimited Pankration U-17 had ended with my brother's victory.

"That was nuts," I said.

"…It *w a s* broken, righ t?" asked the silhouette.

"Yes, he actually used his broken right leg to launch a jaw-cracking kick that gave his enemy a cerebral concussion and won by one-hit KO," I said.

Naturally, no one had expected Shu to do something *that* intense with his injured leg. Gregory certainly hadn't seen it coming and hadn't been ready to guard against it, letting my brother land a clean hit.

"...Unfai r."

"You can say *that* again," I said. He'd made all the sympathy he'd gotten from the audience go to waste.

Now that I think about it, it was kinda suspicious how the very reason for that sympathy — the news of him getting into that accident — spread throughout the whole venue, I thought. It had allowed him to perform the perfect surprise attack. That was enough reason to believe that Shu had actually done something to make it happen.

And with that in mind, it was possible to assume that even his cheerfulness before the match had actually been a strategic move in preparation for the kick.

Whatever the case, that reckless attack had naturally made the injury worse, extending the recovery period from one month to three months.

Once I'd met my brother after the event, he had put up the most obnoxiously proud face and said something along the lines of "*This* is what it means to give your all to grab hold of the possibility!"

To which I had replied with, "Bro, you idiot! What are you doing?!" while throwing a towel at his face.

Oh yeah, I thought. *That was actually the point when I started calling him "bro."*

"What an inte n s e brother," commented the silhouette.

"Indeed he is," I nodded.

Even though he'd seriously ruined the words he'd said back in the waiting room, they were still etched deep into my heart. That was the reason why I was always ready to reach for the possibility leading me to a future without regret or bad aftertastes.

"That was probably why the replay ended after the talk in the waiting room," I said. The match itself wouldn't have added anything of value.

Though it was probably a good show of his "grab hold of the possibility no matter what it takes" stance, I wasn't the type to take the mentality *that* far. I'd also never thought I'd get into a situation where I'd have to, but…

"Despe r a te times, desperate m e a sures," said the silhouette.

"Yeah," I said.

With the memory replay being over, I was about to wake up. Once that happened, I would have to face Gouz-Maise in an even worse situation than before. Thus, if I was going to seize the possibility, I'd have to get some new methods.

"Well, I'll have a go at it, anyway," I said.

"I s ee," nodded the silhouette. "The n, wake up."

It seemed to me as though the entity smiled.

"Ray, hav e a question?"

Well, there's one thing I want to know, I thought.

"All right, I'll ask directly… What are you?" My own conjecture wasn't enough to figure out its identity.

"…Eheh e h." I couldn't see any eyes on the dark red silhouette, but I could easily tell that it looked into mine and laughed. "You wo n 't mas ter me if you on l y use the flames, Ray."

Those words were enough for me to understand what the entity was. "Y-You're Gardran...?"

Before I could finish that sentence, the world of dreams began to fade.

"I am a fragment. A power left unused because of you defeating us while we were incomplete. I am the life and mind that the demon failed to birth. The life that was reborn as your item. I am the 'me' that wants to know the man who slaughtered my mother."

The silhouette — Gardranda — spoke while its appearance gradually became less vague. Its form wasn't that of the great demon, but that of a small girl with horns.

"I understand you now," she said. "So please, understand *me*, too."

And so, our world of memories and dreams began fade.

"Wake up, use all you have, including me and Nemesis, and grab hold of the possibility, okay?" She spoke those words, and reality came flooding back.

Maiden of Vengeance, Nemesis

As I had evaded its attacks and used feints, I'd bought about five minutes of time. My body was covered in many light wounds. Though I was able to dodge its legs and fists, I was getting damaged by the pieces of the ground and trees that it shattered.

Though it hurt to admit it — my non-weapon form was weak. Since I had no means of healing myself, I wouldn't last long.

Gouz-Maise, on the other hand, was completely unharmed. Since my blade couldn't even give it as much as a scratch, it didn't even need to use Automatic Restoration.

"B o U s y u S s A d a S A A   a a A!" Even though it wasn't hurt, Gouz-Maise was irritated that it couldn't kill me and expressed it by letting out enraged roars and secreting some indescribable bile from the faces all over its body.

The sight was downright vile.

The creature was the very embodiment of the vileness involved in any gathering of corpses. Both its appearance and way of existing were revolting enough to turn the very sight of it into something that made my mind creak. That was how I felt about undead in general.

Back when Ray and I had visited the Tomb Labyrinth, I'd been scared beyond words. I didn't know why, but undead were extremely dreadful to me. When looking through Ray's memories for an answer, I'd thought that I was simply weak to horror.

However, that wasn't it. I had come to understand it after facing the undead in the dungeon and the abomination before me. I wasn't afraid of their appearances. What I found dreadful was their very existence.

They were dead, yet they didn't go to any afterlife, nor were they reborn.

They were dead, yet they continued to walk among us.

That nightmarish state was so frightening it made my heart tighten.

I didn't know the reason why.

However, my heart was telling me that I simply couldn't let it continue on like this.

"My heart, eh?" I murmured.

How peculiar, I thought. *According to Ray's knowledge, I am nothing but an AI inside a game. Do I really have a heart? Wait.*

"At the very least, I have enough of it to feel one thing," I said.

It was certainly there. I had a heart that felt something for Ray.

"Heh heh." I couldn't help but laugh. There was no denying that it was quite comical. After all — he was the very cause of my existence. Yet, the way my heart felt about him was no falsehood.

I...

"D A s d a S A A a A a a a A!"

"You just *had* to ruin the moment, didn't you, you uncouth lout?" I snapped.

Lengthy protrusions squirmed out of several mouths all over Gouz-Maise's body.

They were tongues. The rot dripping down from them wasn't the only thing suggesting that they were quite unlike those of humans — their very shape was reminiscent of the tongues used by chameleons or frogs from Ray's memory.

It was obvious what it was planning to use them for.

Clearly, it had grown sick and tired of my constant evasion. Much like snakes raising their heads, the tongues were readied to strike at me.

"I won't be able to dodge this," I said. Not only was I injured — I simply didn't have the skill and ability to evade such an attack. There was no way for me to stall it any longer.

"...Heh heh."

Look at me, Ray, I thought. *This is how strong I am by my lonesome. This is the extent of what I can do when I'm just by myself. While alone, I can't go any farther than this. So...*

"So just come here already."

The moment Gouz-Maise was about to pierce me with its tongues…

"Sure."

…I heard that single word, which was followed by a stream of dark red fire that burned the fleshy extensions.

The fire on its tongues made Gouz-Maise wail in anguish. At this point, the blazing, dark red flames were familiar to me. After all, the one commanding them was my Master.

"You sure took your time, Ray," I said.

"Sorry, a little dream made me oversleep," he replied.

"You shouldn't keep a lady waiting too long," I scolded. "But, well… you made it in time, so I don't mind."

"Thanks, Nemesis."

Hearing that made my expression turn softer, but I made a conscious effort not to show it.

"So, shall we continue?" I asked. "We're out of Absorption uses and have wounds all over us. The situation is worse than before. Do you think we can do it?"

"Yeah," Ray nodded. "I remembered something… no, two things. We'll use them to defeat this thing."

"Remembered two things? Care to share?"

Before answering my question, Ray wore an intrepid grin. "Something I neglected to use… and my brother's words."

The moment he said that, I instantly understood what he was thinking and came to know his plan.

Oh my, I thought, both impressed and slightly shocked.

"Heh heh! Are you insane?" I asked.

"Nope," he answered.

"This will be an act of pure madness with a low probability of success. It will be as dangerous as a walk on a tightrope, won't it?!" I was thoroughly puzzled by his thought process.

"If the possibility is there, I'll just give my all to seize it," he said.

I see, I thought. *Then I shall accompany you.*

"Though, the chance of this plan leading us to victory is about... 30%, and that's being generous," he added.

About a third, eh?

"Seems enough to me," I said.

"More than enough," Ray agreed. After that exchange, I took my sword form and became Ray's weapon.

"Let's win, shall we?" I said.

"Yeah, let's win."

And so, turning to face the abomination that was Gouz-Maise, Ray and I became one.

Revenant Ox-Horse, Gouz-Maise

The creature the world proclaimed to be "Revenant Ox-Horse, Gouz-Maise" was enraged.

Since the moment it'd been born, Gouz-Maise had felt only indescribable amounts of hatred. That was because the creature was an actual amalgam of the rage and resentment left behind by the deceased. It was the *result* of those who had left nothing else behind but regret.

"G U d s F D g a a d A S a a A A a A d S d A A a!"

That was *all* that Gouz-Maise was.

The dead that were its base were those who had lived by avarice and vice — people who had failed to leave behind anything but their grudge. If at least one of those inside had died with love in their heart, this amalgam of death probably wouldn't have grown this powerful and might not have become a UBM. But alas, that hadn't happened, and Gouz-Maise — as it was now — would never reflect upon itself. The grudge boiling within the creature was enraging it, compelling it to use its might against the living and forcing them to join the grudgeful chaos within it.

However, at this point in time, Gouz-Maise was even more enraged than usual. That was because the puny, mouse-like living creature below it couldn't die.

It was a Master.

Masters were immortal.

Killing them just made them momentarily disappear. However — that was the extent of it. These living creatures would simply brush off that transient death as if it was nothing and then just continue existing.

This one, in particular, had faced Gouz-Maise and tried to prevent it from drowning other living creatures into its grudge.

Even if hurt, left alone, or shattered with a punch, the Master would continue getting in its way.

Gouz-Maise couldn't stomach that. It didn't have a mind to understand why, but it just couldn't tolerate that Master.

However, it was about to be over. Gouz-Maise had a means of ending it. It was a powerful spell used by one of those who'd become the creature. The undead intended to finally kill the Master by casting it once again.

Once that was done, it intended to go to town. A significant part of its grudge wished to kill the people inhabiting the places within its memory and make them join the grudge within it. It believed that — in doing so — it could become more powerful and thus become able to sink even more living creatures into its grudge. And it would continue until the whole world was sunk.

Yes... yeah, I... we are all dead here. So, a world where people still live is a mistake. It's... wrong, it's so wrong! All of it, all of it, all of it, all of it, all of it must sink into the abyss. Kill and consume everything there is in this world.

Gouz-Maise's consciousness was like a colored marble that mixed objectivity and subjectivity. Chaotic as its mind was, however, it could still become puzzled. Not by its own thoughts, obviously, but by the actions of the puny one below.

The puny one used his left hand to push a cloth against his mouth... while the bracer on his right was directed at Gouz-Maise.

Those bracers released fire. Gouz-Maise already knew that much. However, so far, only the left bracer had released the flames, and it had no recollection of the right one ever doing the same.

As Gouz-Maise's chaotic mind tried to figure out what the right bracer released...

"Hellish Miasma... full power!"

...the blond man declared something, making a dark purple smoke gush out of his right bracer with great intensity.

Gouz-Maise wasn't familiar with this attack. It didn't know what it was, its effects, or what the enemy was planning. Using its limited reasoning power, Gouz-Maise tried to understand what it was, and it didn't take long for it to come to a conclusion.

The smoke was harmless to it — beneficial, even.

It was miasma. A poisonous mist that afflicted, weakened, and led the living through a slow death.

To Gouz-Maise — an undead — it wasn't much of a problem.

Because it had living cells, it couldn't avoid the debuffs, but their impact on its body was insignificant. In the first place, slight amounts of Weakness and Intoxication were meaningless against an amalgam of corpses. Even if Gouz-Maise received the debuffs, their effect was negligible. Though Poison damaged its cells, it wasn't anything that couldn't be taken care of by its Automatic Restoration.

Thus, because it only pushed living people closer to death, the miasma was a net positive for Gouz-Maise. Trying to figure out why the man had done something so foolish, it finally became aware of a certain fact.

It couldn't see anything. The dark purple smoke had spread all the way up to the base of its throat, and not even the use of the eyes on the faces all over its body could help it make sense of the surroundings.

This smokescreen was exactly what the man had intended. Even though the miasma was dangerous to him, he'd used it regardless just to hinder Gouz-Maise's vision.

"D a a D F d Z f a a A S s a D A S a s A a A a a A A!"   Gouz-Maise roared and began rampaging wildly. Its ground-shattering, indiscriminate movements were meant to crush the man, who was surely still around. Gouz-Maise kept stomping for a while — not minding the damage it was doing to both the surface and the faces on its legs — yet it didn't feel anything living under its feet.

It couldn't hit the man. Nor did it know where he was. That situation made it both angry and uneasy, but within its chaotic grudge, there was a composed part that came to a certain conclusion.

The man is aiming for the head. However, he's both puny and cannot fly. To attack the head, he will try to cut the legs. At that moment, we must cast the ultimate spell and kill him along with the limb he attacks.

The plan involved sacrificing a part of itself. However, due to Gouz-Maise possessing Automatic Restoration, it wasn't a heavy price. Even if the man had hidden himself, there was still only one way for him to emerge victorious. As long as Gouz-Maise didn't let him do that, its victory was assured. The man could still use the flames, but they only gave it pain and never came close to being fatal.

Next moment... The next moment we feel pain, we will launch the spell towards it, thought Gouz-Maise. *The cost of using it a second time is heavy. However, it's a small price to pay to kill him.*

With those thoughts, it focused its attention on its legs and gave the body's control to the grudge that could use the spell.

Then, it exposed the core in its head and readied itself to cast the magic.

Suddenly, Gouz-Maise's back left leg was touched, causing its semi-rotten neural system to send it a signal.

"D E e e E a A D d L y y Y y M i x e E E e e R r r R R R r R!!"

A moment later, it launched the spell with the intention to disintegrate both the man and its own leg.

The speed at which it had turned its head to do that caused the rotten skin on its neck to rip and shred apart, but it didn't care. Though its aim was extremely forced, the power of the attack was great enough to make its back left leg disappear. Gouz-Maise lost its footing and screamed due to the searing pain it felt, but the damage wasn't something that couldn't be handled by its restorative ability.

What's important is that we killed hi—

The second that thought went through its head, the man that was supposed to be disintegrated jumped up on Gouz-Maise's back.

It couldn't understand what had happened. Countless grudges within it became astir and caused it to momentarily stiffen.

Then, it noticed the man's state.

His right hand was covered in blood and held a familiar piece of flesh. It was a part of Gouz-Maise's body, and — by looking at his mouth — it was easy to tell that he'd *taken a bite of it*. Lastly, he held a halberd with a black flag flying behind its ax blade.

Just now, with abnormal swiftness, he'd jumped on Gouz-Maise's back, and he was now getting ready to charge towards its head. His speed was far greater than it had been a few moments ago, or even when he'd been completely unhurt. It was hard to believe that he was heavily hurt. In fact, his wounds were disappearing right before its eyes.

Suddenly, the grudge that controlled Gouz-Maise shuddered with fear. After all — it was reminiscent of the chase back in the dungeon.

"Looks like... it worked," said the man through his ragged breath. The deathly faces all over its body heard the man's mutter. "If you get a debuff by eating a part of a debuffed opponent's body... Reversal recognizes it as a negative effect caused by the enemy. That was proven by the Grapevine I fought this morning."

Gouz-Maise didn't understand what the man was saying.

"I didn't know if Hellish Miasma had any effect on undead, and there was a chance that the thing with the Grapevine only happened because it was caused by its attack," the man said. "If that was the case, I'd have ended up dying from my own attack... but it worked."

Gouz-Maise couldn't make sense of the man's current state.

"Ha ha… What a disgusting gamble," the man laughed.

Gouz-Maise just barely had enough mind to understand that the man had created this situation by consuming its rotten flesh.

"G g i i l i i e E e!?   D d G g A a a A A a A q Q a A a!?" it screamed through its head and all the mouths all over its body.

"You scared?" the man asked.

Indeed — Gouz-Maise was afraid. All as one, the consensus of the Gouz-Maise Gang — the group of scoundrels that had taken many lives and consumed great amounts of human flesh — feared the man before them.

"Guess it's the first time *you've* gotten eaten, huh," the man said. This was the man who, as if to give it payback for its sins, had consumed Gouz-Maise's flesh and drawn ever closer to end its deathless life.

Naturally, the amalgam of undead was afraid of the way the man functioned.

He was truly a God of Death.

His hands — one blood crimson, other a deathly black — held a dark flag. On his head, there were wolf-like ears. He didn't hesitate to consume the flesh of man-eaters. If he wasn't the reaper sent himself to end them — no one was.

"K A d s F a!? A s a S A D a a A q A S Q a!"

Gouz-Maise began wildly swinging its arms down at him, but the man was able to evade it all, making it seem as though the amalgam of corpses had become pitifully sluggish. Not only that — he jumped on the left arm it swung down and began running up towards its head.

Little by little, the god of death... the Grim Reaper... the ultimate end... approached Gouz-Maise.

Overwhelmed by despair, it used its final card.

"D e E e A A — D e E a a D A a a — D d d D L Y y y M i X e E e e E E r r R R r R !?!?"

That was the third time it cast the ultimate spell.

It didn't care about what would happen because of that. Since the spell consumed great amounts of grudge — which was the core of Gouz-Maise's being — there was a chance that using it thrice in such a short period of time could made itself self-destruct. However, its fear of the man running up its arm was just too great for it to hold back.

The burst of destructive magic made the god of death and everything below the elbow completely vanish. Though Gouz-Maise's arm was thicker than a large tree, the spell disintegrated even its bones.

The pain signals were abnormally powerful, and due to the loss of its grudge, its Automatic Restoration didn't work at full capacity. The grudge flowing through its corpus was reduced to just that of the one who could cast Deadly Mixer and a few others. Despite that, however, the faces covering its body and the few remaining grudges all smiled in relief.

One leg, one arm, and approximately 80% of the grudge composing it.

The losses were great, but they had been enough to make their bane — the reaper himself — disappear. The battle was over. Now, it simply had to wait for the Automatic Restoration to complete, head to town to stock up on new grudge and...

"A a H h H h?" All of a sudden, a shadow came over it from above its head.

Gouz-Maise looked upwards.

Before the sunset, bathed in the light of the sinking sun, there was the source of the shadow.

The black silhouette held a black sword in the hand behind him. And, with great speed, he closed in towards Gouz-Maise's head.

"You beasts, wallowing in undeath..." a feminine voice began.

"...go to sleep... forever!" the Reaper finished.

The tip of the black greatsword pierced through Gouz-Maise's forehead and touched its core.

"VENGEANCE IS MINE!"

Thus, a strike worth all the damage Gouz-Maise had ever given the man... no — a retributive attack avenging all the people that had suffered because of those composing the amalgam of death...

...completely destroyed its core and ended its very existence.

Undisclosed Location

["Maw of the Desert, Azmore" was defeated]
[Final level: 56]
[MVP: "The Earth" Fatoum, level 1,157 (total level: 1,657)]
[Embryo: "Overflowing Divine Vessel, The Grail"]
[MVP special reward: Legendary item, "Bag of the Desert, Azmore"]

■

["The Crimson Armor, Exademon" was defeated]
[Final level: 63]
[MVP: "King of Termination" Albert Schwartzkaiser, level 620 (total level: 1,120)]
[Embryo: "Seven Star Turnover, Septentrion"]
[MVP special reward: Ancient Legendary item, "Crimson Armor-Piercer, Exademon"]

■

["Four-Dimensional Kaiju, Todoghilas"]
[Final level: 51]
[MVP: "Commander-in-Chief" Gray α Centauri, level 490 (total level: 990)]
[Embryo: "Unidentified Flying Stronghold, Laputa"]

[MVP special reward: Ancient Legendary item, "Ultimate Suit Series, Todoghilas"]

◾

["Revenant Ox-Horse, Gouz-Maise"]
[Final level: 34]
[MVP: "Paladin" Ray Starling, level 35 (total level: 35)]
[Embryo: "Maiden of Vengeance, Nemesis"]
[MVP special reward: Epic item, "Grudge-soaked Greaves, Gouz-Maise"]

"...Hm?"

In a space enlightened by countless data windows, *it* sounded a voice of confusion.

At first glance, it appeared to be an adult male human, but upon further inspection, one would notice that the skin covering its body had patches of draconic scales and beastly leather, while its head was decorated by devilish horns. Overall, it certainly looked more like a "humanoid monster" than a person, but the glasses it sported successfully moved the impression it gave off into the "human" territory — if only barely.

It was doing one of the jobs it was assigned to — the checking of the data concerning the defeat of UBMs over a set period of time. In *Infinite Dendrogram*, its role was the acknowledgement of UBMs.

Though UBMs were abnormally powerful and had abilities just as strong, their primary unique feature was their transformation into special rewards upon defeat.

Many non-UBM boss monsters also had great strength and unique abilities. When defeated — either by people or other monsters — they dropped Treasure Coffers or items they possessed before death.

However, the special rewards left by UBMs were completely unlike any basic boss monster drops. They were the materializations of the image — the concepts — surrounding the abilities of the defeated UBM, adjusted to best suit the most valuable person in the battle.

Indeed, it wasn't their strength or abilities. That very transformation was the prime feature of UBMs.

No standard monster possessed it. But if the control AI responsible for UBMs acknowledged a unit as a UBM, it would become exactly that — a monster with the function to transform into a special reward upon death.

The creature working in this space was Jabberwock — the very same control AI responsible for acknowledging, giving features to, and sometimes even designing UBMs.

"'Ray Starling,'" it murmured. "Going by Earth time, I saw this player name yesterday."

It was the very same player that had, at an unreasonably low level, defeated the Great Miasmic Hobgoblin, Gardranda — a UBM of Jabberwock's design. Naturally, Jabberwock was slightly surprised to see the same person become an MVP in a UBM fight two days in a row.

In this world, the UBMs Jabberwock had either designed or acknowledged were many. However, the same couldn't be said for MVPs.

Many people couldn't defeat them. Others couldn't even encounter them. Others just plain couldn't become MVPs.

Not to mention that the strongest of the strong — Superiors — were actively hunting UBMs. As a result, only the few lucky enough to encounter *and* successfully defeat them could become MVPs.

Thus, Jabberwock was quite intrigued by an entity that had faced UBMs two days in a row and — through hard struggles — emerged victorious both times.

"Fascinating," it said. "If only most defeated UBMs like he did. I'm quite dissatisfied by how Superiors hunt them as if it's a chore. Truly, treasure is best when earned through harsh struggles and intense drama. No good saga or epic is complete without those things, after all." Jabberwock continuously nodded to his own words before beginning to ponder. "I believe I should make my designs even more tenacious."

Saying that, he closed his eyes in thought…

"Let's start by giving it atomic breath. Like Godzilla."

The moment Jabberwock said something truly foreboding, something gave a response. "No radioactive pollution, pleease!" Before he'd realized it, a cat-like mascot was sitting in the space behind him.

It was Cheshire — control AI no. 13. Shaking its head at just how troublesome its colleague was, it began commenting about what Jabberwock was trying to do.

"Leave the unreasonable amounts of power to SUBMs. They create enough calamities as it iis. We don't need anything that could cause irregular evolutioon. Do you have any idea how much trouble we had with the last two irregularrs? Even Humpty's favorite and Granvaloa's Superiors could barely stop the Corpse Stronghold, while the Disaster Bioweapon is still space-sealed in Red King's 'gaol,' you know? The ones who do all the work to take care of your UBMs are the tians, us, and the players, you know?"

"I'm aware," said Jabberwock. "Now, what is your business here, thirteen?"

"Oh yeah, I almost forgot," said Cheshire. "The control AI responsible for monsters, Queen, has a message for you."

"Which is…?"

"'Explain your previous acknowledgement.'"

"What am I supposed to make of that?" Jabberwock demanded.

"She gave me a letter, but — just as you'd expect from her — it was both overly emotional and too verbose, so I shortened iit," said Cheshire. "Also, it's about Gouz-Maise — the last monster you acknowledged as a UBM."

"I see." That was enough for Jabberwock to understand Queen's problem.

"If I had to add a bit more detail to that, it'd be, 'It wasn't born naturally, nor was it created or arranged by us. Why are you giving UBM status to an undead born from human sorceryy?'"

"Gouz-Maise had interesting unique abilities," said Jabberwock. "Its stats and the circumstances behind its birth were more than enough to give it Epic status. Also, by looking at the series of events that led to its creation, it's safe to say that there will never be another Gouz-Maise."

Thus, Jabberwock believed that acknowledging it as a UBM had made perfect sense.

"That's truue," said Cheshire. "Queen is probably just complaining because she's upset that not many of the boss monsters she singled out and improved are being acknowledged as UBMs."

"I'm just doing my job," replied Jabberwock. "Also, does it actually matter to us whether I acknowledge something as a UBM or not?"

"...I think she's just being peevish because she doesn't feel appreciateed," said Cheshire. "But oh weell."

While thinking about the relationship between this thickheaded fellow AI and the Queen, Cheshire heaved a sigh.

"Also, no. 3's designs are unrefined at best, and overly predictable, at worst. Too lacking in both inventiveness and potential," added Jabberwock. "When it comes to those points, this Gouz-Maise creature and some player designs make far better UBMs."

"Queen is a simple and straightforward girl, after aall... Wait, what?" Cheshire realized that Jabberwock had just said something that simply couldn't be ignored. "Player designs? What do you mean?"

"Exactly what I said," said Jabberwock. "I'm talking about that Superior from Dryfe."

"...Ohh." The mention of that single person was more than enough for Cheshire. The Superior in question was more than capable of creating a monster that could catch Jabberwock's eye.

"A part of me feels like Ray will get involved in thaat," said Cheshire.

There was no basis for the cat's assumption. One could write it off as standard intuition, but with the control AIs all having calculational capabilities that no human could match, it was difficult to call it "standard."

Jabberwock wondered why Cheshire's mutter had included the name of the player he'd been intrigued by just a moment ago, but chose not to react to it in any meaningful way.

The cat in question, on the other hand, became curious about something relating to its own murmur and chose to ask about it. "Oh, yeah. Thinking of Ray made me remember. Hey, Jabberwock."

"Yes?"

"Remember the 'Great Miasmic Hobgoblin, Gardranda' that he defeated recently?" said Cheshire. "What would've happened if it had reached completion? It died when it was only in its second form, so I'm kinda curious."

I know it's my own fault for telling Ray its weak point, but still, it thought.

In response...

"It would've been born."

...Jabberwock said something far too concise.

"...Sorry, but I don't get iit," said Cheshire.

So concise, in fact, that not even an AI with inhuman calculational capabilities could make sense of it.

"Its final form was the creature that was supposed to be born based on the demon's accumulated fighting experience," elaborated Jabberwock.

"A separate unit?" asked Cheshire.

"No." The UBM control AI shook his head. "It's better to look at it this way: the 'mother' was only a cover, and the child that was supposed to be born was the true Gardranda. Sadly, it didn't get a chance to reveal itself."

Power left unused — a life and mind that had failed to be birthed. That was exact same thing that the silhouette in Ray's dream — the non-mother Gardranda — had told him.

So that's why the demon's weak point was the stomaach, Cheshire thought and nodded to itself. "By the way, what kind of creature would it have been born aas?"

"If I recall correctly, the mother fought and ate primarily humans," said Jabberwock. "Thus, it's fair to assume that it would've been humanoid."

"It's also fair to assume that it won't get another chance at being born, riight?" Cheshire asked.

"Yes, indeed."

However, Jabberwock thought to himself, *that might change depending on the final skill it received when it became an item.*

There was a chance that the effect of the skill Ray had yet to unlock could give another chance to the creature that'd failed to be birthed. However, due to there not being any similar cases, Jabberwock concluded that it was highly unlikely.

"Now, if you'll excuse me, I have work to return to," he said.

"Sure, I have some tasks to do, tooo."

Jabberwock ended the conversation and faced a window displaying a stream of information.

Cheshire left his colleague's work area and went to do his own work.

Paladin Ray Starling

[UBM, "Revenant Ox-Horse, Gouz-Maise" was defeated]
[Selecting MVP]
[Ray Starling was selected as MVP]

[Ray Starling is presented with an MVP special reward — "Grudge-soaked Greaves, Gouz-Maise"]

"So that's done, huh…?" I murmured.

With Gouz-Maise's body disintegrating into particles of light and me receiving a message window similar to the one I'd gotten after defeating Gardranda, I could finally be relieved that I'd killed the abomination. However, my situation didn't allow it. After all, since Gouz-Maise was about forty meters tall, defeating it from the head had left me to fall the entire way down.

Not to mention that I couldn't move my body, either.

To win this fight, I'd used a downright insane method of activating Like a Flag Flying the Reversal. Thanks to the debuffs I'd received getting turned into buffs, I had become more powerful than I was at my best, and had been able to emerge victorious against the abomination. However, just like it had been with Gardranda, the switching of weapons or the defeat of the enemy, Gouz-Maise, had caused the skill to get canceled. Thus, I was left burdened with a number of debuffs. My status window displayed Poison, Weakness, and Intoxication — the three effects of Hellish Miasma — along with Curse and Food Poisoning, which I'd most likely gotten for ingesting Gouz-Maise's flesh.

Well, I ate a part of a goddamn undead's body, so I can't really be surprised, I thought.

Moments after I canceled the Reversal by switching Nemesis to her sword form, I was able to move my body long enough to activate Vengeance is Mine, but the debuffs had gotten worse since then. I could no longer move so much as a muscle.

As things were, I was seconds away from crashing to the ground, and I would be able to do nothing to break my fall. With my current HP and the general state of my body, it was highly questionable if I could survive the hit.

"Better say my prayers, then…" I murmured.

A moment after I closed my eyes and braced myself for impact, I felt the touch of something unnaturally light.

The sensation repeated a couple of times. After the gentle swaying, I felt my body land on the ground.

I was thoroughly confused.

Fearfully, I opened my eyes and saw a shining artificial horse, Silver, standing at my side. Just like the first time I'd fallen off of him, he was looking down at me, seemingly worried.

It was apparent that Silver had gently caught me as I'd fallen and softly dropped me to the ground. I had no idea how he'd done it with his equestrian frame, but there was no other explanation.

"Ha ha," I laughed. "Thanks, Silver."

Not being an animal, he had no mouth and thus couldn't make any natural sounds, so he responded to my gratitude by simply rubbing the end of his "nose" on my cheek. That action made him seem much like a real horse.

With how he'd helped me chase down the Lich, it was safe to say that Silver had been an invaluable asset in this event. And if I hadn't had the Miasmaflame Bracers and hadn't seen that dream, there would have been a large chance of me losing this fight. However, there was someone who'd done more to help me than anyone else.

"Thanks, Nemesis," I said. "If you hadn't persisted like you did, it would've all been over for us."

If I hadn't had Nemesis and she hadn't bought the time I'd needed to regain my consciousness, I'd have been given the death penalty, and that pile of corpses would've been free to attack someone else. Nemesis was the sole reason why that hadn't happened, so I expressed my thanks.

However, all I got in response was peaceful, systematic breathing. Before I knew it, she'd disappeared from my weapon equipment slot, returned to her humanoid form, and had fallen fast asleep. It reminded me of a similar moment back in the dragon carriage after the battle with Gardranda.

The peace in her expression felt like the ultimate proof of the hard work she'd done today.

"Well done... Nemesis." I touched her with my left hand, causing her to instantly return to the crest.

Left alone and unable to move, I kept my HP up by casting healing magic on myself, and looked through my items to find a way how to neutralize the status effects. The misadventure from today's morning had made me learn my lesson, so I'd prepared for the three Hellish Miasma debuffs by buying the appropriate items when shopping.

After taking those, I lessened the effects of Food Poisoning by vomiting a few times, and made it go away completely by following that up with a swig of the right medicine.

The last status effect — Curse — went away by itself as I was busy taking care of the others.

Since I hadn't gotten attacked at all while doing any of that, I assumed that Gouz-Maise's rampage had probably caused all the local monsters to scatter, letting me completely heal myself and remove the debuffs completely unbothered.

Even though my status screen now said that I was in perfect shape, I certainly didn't feel like it. The entire time interval from the moment I'd infiltrated the fortress until I'd ended the battle with Gouz-Maise had been a great drain on my mental and physical energy. My HP might've been at 100%, but I wasn't confident if I could wring up even 60% of my usual performance. Not to mention that Nemesis was in no state to fight, either.

Anyway, it was as good a time as any to check out the MVP special reward I'd gotten from Gouz-Maise.

As it said in the name, the "Grudge-soaked Greaves" were a pair of boots made of a malicious-looking purple metal and some leather — hopefully not human leather — and its description in the window went like so:

[Grudge-soaked Greaves, Gouz-Maise]
[Epic Item]
An epic item embodying the concepts surrounding the ox-headed horse-man clad in grudge.
In addition to converting surrounding negative emotions into pure power, it grants the wearer an understanding of the unity between man and horse.
[This item cannot be transferred or traded.]

"'Epic Item'?" Those were the first words that escaped my lips once I saw the status screen.

Given that the Miasmaflame Bracers, Gardranda was a "Legendary Item," I was now curious about what kind of difference those descriptions referred to.

I looked through the help window and found a section on "MVP special reward ranks." I couldn't recall it being there the last time I checked over this general area of help sections, so I could only assume that it had appeared there only recently. If I had to guess, it had probably appeared there after I'd acquired the Miasmaflame Bracers.

As for the content of the help section, it said that UBMs and the MVP special rewards received upon defeating them had several ranks. Those ranks were primarily decided based on the UBM's strength and threat level, and from lowest to highest, they went like so: Epic, Legendary, Ancient Legendary, Mythical, and Superior.

Though I'd gotten stronger since my battle with the demon, I still felt that Gouz-Maise had been more challenging than Gardranda. However, the rank on the Miasmaflame Bracers was above that of the new special reward.

The stat bonuses reflected that, as well. While the Grudge-soaked Greaves increased my AGI by 30%, Miasmaflame Bracers increased my STR by 100%. Clearly, Gardranda had been above Gouz-Maise.

I felt that she herself might know something about this. After all, she'd called herself "a power left unused" and "the life and mind that the demon failed to birth."

With that in mind, I tried talking to the Miasmaflame Bracers on my hands, but I didn't get any sort of response.

That dream had been more than enough for me to confirm that her mind was still intact, but apparently, she had no means of talking to me in reality.

Suddenly, I was hit with the terrifying idea that Gouz-Maise, too, still had its mind. However, after a moment of consideration,

I concluded that the greaves were completely devoid of any sort of consciousness. Though the assumption was based entirely on intuition alone, for one reason or another, I didn't feel that it was the least bit wrong.

If I had to add reasoning to this, I'd simply say that the boots simply lacked the grudge that had permeated every inch of everything relating to the creature known as Gouz-Maise.

With that settled, I began examining the two skills on the Greaves of Grudge.

The first was Grudge Conversion, which was a downgraded version of the grudge power that had fueled Gouz-Maise. It absorbed the grudge from the surroundings, stored it, and turned it into either SP or MP. Though I assumed it had been part of the monster's functionality, the skill didn't come with the Automatic Restoration ability.

…Upon further thought, I realized that having my lost limbs regrow would be downright freaky, so I was kinda glad it wasn't there.

The second skill — Rider and Horse, As One — was clearly based on the fact that Gouz-Maise had been a horse-man. It increased the Horse Riding skill level by one.

Wait…

Increased the Horse Riding skill level by one.

"I can finally ride Silver!" Overcome with emotion, I shouted out my joy.

This is great, I thought.

It was exactly what I needed to no longer have to ride Silver like I was performing some circus act.

The skill also increased AGI while riding a horse by 10% for every Horse Riding skill level. That was pretty good, too… in fact, that was probably the primary effect of the skill. However, since I hadn't even been able to begin to ride, I appreciated the bonus effect far more.

With that, I got on Silver and began following the road which Hugo and Cyco had used to get to Gideon. I rode the mechanical horse as its hooves rhythmically hit the ground, and I couldn't help but be moved by the fact that I wasn't falling off.

Feeling exceedingly comfortable, I relaxed and head towards Gideon as I let Silver canter as he pleased.

I hope I can run into Hugo along the way, I thought.

More than an hour after equipping the Grudge-soaked Greaves, Silver and I were still on a mountain road.

"Are we there yet…?" I asked no one in particular.

During this time, my Horse Riding skill had already increased by one, and I'd gotten a message saying that the quest "Rescue Roddie Lancarse" was complete. It seemed safe to believe that Hugo had arrived at Gideon and handed the children over to the quest giver girl and the parents. I, too, wished I was in Gideon with them.

"I honestly think we should be close by now," I said. The uncertainty in my tone was due to the fact that I wasn't sure if the road I was following was the correct one.

When going from Gideon to the Gouz-Maise hideout, we had used a Magingear, and — to avoid getting spotted — traversed a path where we wouldn't meet any people. Now, however, I was following a mountain road that was well-maintained enough to not have a single blade of grass growing out of it. When taking my and Silver's comfort into consideration, this path was far better than the former, but it wasn't without its problems, either.

The Cruella Mountain Belt was a net of many roads of various sizes. According to the area's description in the help window, while some of them had been made on the kingdom's or Gideon's orders, many had been randomly created by the local gangs.

With all the magic in this fantasy world, road-related public works weren't a hard task. There were even spells that allowed the caster to make vegetation simply move away, so it might've even been easier than using heavy machinery.

Due to that, there were countless roads, which made it difficult for me — a person with no knowledge of the lay of the land — to find my way back. Since I hadn't gotten to the hideout by taking these mountain paths, my map didn't display which one led to Gideon, and thus didn't help with the pathfinding all that much.

However, since I knew the approximate location of the city, I could make good use of the map window's cardinal directions. With that as my compass, I was able to make my way to where I thought Gideon was.

Considering our speed and the amount of time that had passed, the city should've — at very least — been in sight by now…

"Oh." Just as I thought that, I noticed Gideon's outline peeking through the spaces between the trees.

Since we were still on the mountain, I got to look down at it from a particularly high point. Though it was already turning dark, the city was emitting lots of light, making it obvious that its people were still full of energy.

"Hm?" I murmured.

A certain sound reached my ears. It was the sound of hooves hitting the ground beneath — something I'd grown familiar with throughout today. Except this time, there were many such sounds, and their sources all seemed to be in one group. Not only that — they seemed to be getting closer to me.

"What?"

As I imagined the unlikely and, frankly, silly scenario in which I was being chased by a group of horse-men Liches, the sound suddenly mixed with the sound of metal armor fittings scraping against each other. Soon enough, I saw a group of horses being ridden by people in full plate armor.

It was a highly familiar group — Liliana's Knights of the Royal Guard.

"Hello, Liliana," I said. "We sure see each other a lot to—"

"Ray!" she exclaimed before I could finish. "Are you all right?!"

"...day?" *Okay now, why is she looking at me so intensely? I* thought. *And why are her knights turning all alert and battle-ready? Might I get an explanation?*

"Where is the giant undead?!" she continued. "Were you able to escape it?! Or is it still nearby?!"

...Oh, okay, I get it now.

I first explained Liliana that there was no need to worry, and went on to have an exchange of information with her. She gave me a detailed explanation of what had happened on her end.

After we'd split up at the sweets café, Liliana had gone on to continue her search for the second princess, but come evening, she had received a grim piece of information. One of her people had told her that "The second princess seems to have been kidnapped by a suspicious individual."

Liliana had been aware of the vile deeds committed by the Gouz-Maise Gang, and had concluded that it was entirely possible that the second princess had become another one of their victims.

However, Gouz-Maise Gang's hideout had been in the mountain belt that acted as the border between the kingdom and Caldina. Moving out with larger groups of soldiers could've been seen as an act of war.

That was why Liliana had formed a party comprised only of the best of the best of the Royal Guard, and planned a raid rescue mission to the Gouz-Maise Gang's hideout.

The moment they had prepared themselves and began heading out, two carriages had entered Gideon.

Due to it being late, the speed at which they'd entered had made them stand out. Once Liliana had asked them to state their identity and business, the coachman, a Master, had told them something that was nothing short of surprising.

He had said, "I am a Master who accepted the request of one of this city's citizens to rescue a kidnapped boy. We exterminated the gang and brought back all the children that were still alive. However, as we did that, some strange sorcery made the corpses of the gang merge into a giant undead UBM. We were able to escape using the carriages, but my fellow Master is still holding the beast off somewhere in the mountain belt."

The story had been so absurd that some knights simply hadn't believed it. However, a knight with the Truth Discernment skill had concluded that the Master wasn't lying. Not to mention that the requester — who'd been waiting for them by the gates — had confirmed that it was all true.

The shift from a kidnapping event to a UBM assault had made their situation turn quite chaotic. Also, Liliana had gone on to ask for the name of the Master holding back the UBM, causing her to find out that it was someone she was highly familiar with — me.

She had hastily departed the moment she'd found that out. The knights that had been supposed to join her in the rescue operation had gone after her. Some time after that, they'd run into me, still on edge and ready to face the UBM.

"I see," I said. "So Hugo safely got the children to the city. What a relief."

I'd known it from the message I'd received, but now that I'd been told the circumstances surrounding it, I could be certain that there was no need for worry.

"What do you mean, 'What a relief?!'" Liliana exclaimed. "What happened to the UBM?!"

"I defeated it," I curtly answered.

"Oh, I see, so you... you defeated it?!"

"Here." I showed her my boots and opened their informational window.

"...Ray, if I am not mistaken, you became a Paladin about a week ago and were only level 0 before that, correct?" she asked.

"That seems about right," I said. Time went thrice as fast here, after all.

"Why are you able to defeat an UBM a mere week after starting?! Also, I just realized, but those bracers are...!"

"Oh. Yes. I got these the day before yesterday..." Saying that, I showed her the Miasmaflame Bracers, Gardranda.

Liliana froze solid.

"The scale of what they're talking about is just ludicrous," muttered one of the knights to the others. "The only person I know who can defeat a UBM by his lonesome is our late commander."

"You need to be kind of insane to even attempt it, honestly," said another.

"This is just off. Our vice commander is forced to act out the 'straight man' type of character," commented the third knight. "I mean, she's normally the 'natural airhead' type, isn't she?"

"Hhaahh..." sighed Liliana. "Truly, common sense does not apply to you Masters."

"Well, it's not like I won just because of my own abilities," I said. "I had my comrades, lady luck, this horse named Silver, and Nemesis with me."

"Speaking of Nemesis, where is she now?" Lilliana asked.

"She's currently resting," I said. "The things she had to do left her completely drained."

I unequipped the Miasmaflame Bracers and gently rubbed the crest on my left hand, where Nemesis was sleeping.

"Ray... Nemesis..." Liliana spoke again. "I cannot express how valuable your actions are. Because of you, the awful series of kidnappings in Gideon are over and the UBM disaster was prevented. I believe I speak for all the people of the city when I give you my gratitude. Thank you very much."

"Well..." I had trouble reacting to that. "It just happened to turn out this way, for some reason."

I had accepted a quest, gone to save a child, gotten mentally overwhelmed by the tragic sight in the dungeon, let my fury drive me into killing the Lich, and gone on to struggle against the Revenant

Ox-Horse. Seriously, I was completely confused as to why things had turned out this way.

Thinking back on it, there had been events which got me all choked up. I'd felt both deathly dread and disgust. My heart had burned with a fire strong enough to sear my very being.

However, once I'd found out that the children had all returned to the city, safe and sound, the aftertaste of this whole event had become a bit better.

Once we were done with the information exchange, we grouped up and made our way back to Gideon.

Since there was no need to worry about any UBM attacks, Liliana and her knights decided to accompany me. Apparently, she'd noticed how tired I was and had chosen to see to it that I returned to Gideon safely. I highly appreciated that.

"...Ah."

Suddenly, a certain question went through my mind.

"By the way, what happened with the search for Her Highness the princess?" I asked. "I appreciate your company, but shouldn't you be focusing on that, instead...?"

My questions made Liliana's expression turn stiff. At the same time, I felt a strong air of nervousness envelop the other knights.

D-Did I say something bad? I thought.

"Based on what you told me, Her Highness was kidnapped by the gang, right?" I continued. "I didn't get a chance to take a look at the faces of the children in the carriages, so..."

"Her Highness wasn't in the carriages." Liliana's voice as she said that seemed somewhat... flat.

"Does that mean that...?" I asked slowly.

Are there actually more gang members? Did they take her to some other area in the mountains…?

"The kidnapping itself was misinformation," she said. "A short while ago, one of our people contacted me via communication magic and told me that she'd returned home, safe and sound."

"That's grea—"

"I was also told that she was carrying a store-bought mask, sweets, a goldfish, and a painting. She looked thoroughly satisfied."

"I… uh…"

"The one thing she said to the people of the place she is staying at was, 'It was most riveting!'"

I was dumbfounded.

…Your Highness, could you please read the mood? I thought. *These people spent the entire day searching for you.*

Though the way she'd explained the situation to me was highly smooth and matter-of-fact, I could see Lilliana's forehead twitching in anger.

"Ehehehehehehеheh…" she laughed ominously.

"A-Ahahahahahahah…" I reluctantly joined her.

"Ehehehehehehеheh… Let us change the subject."

"Good idea."

Both the mood of the situation and my very instincts told me that delving into this was a bad idea.

We switched to doing some idle chatter and continued following the road towards Gideon.

When we finally reached the city, I couldn't help but notice that its atmosphere was exactly the same as it had been back when I'd entered it for the first time. One of Liliana's fellow knights used a communication magic skill to inform the guards about the defeat of the Epic-rank UBM — Revenant Ox-Horse, Gouz-Maise — causing them to no longer stand on alert.

Once we passed the gates, I looked around, but Hugo and Cyco were nowhere in sight.

"Liliana, there's something I'd like to ask you," I spoke up. "Have you seen Hugo...? He's my comrade. The guy who brought the carriages with the children here."

"Do forgive me," she said. "I ran out the second he told me of the situation. Give me a moment to ask about him."

After saying that, Liliana began speaking to the guards stationed around the gates.

A moment later, one of them took a step forward. "After explaining the situation and handing the children over to us, the person in question said, 'I must return to the other side' and vanished."

Vanished? I asked myself. *What did he mean by "other side"? Dryfe? No...*

"So he logged out, huh?" I said. He'd probably done it to avoid getting questions he wasn't allowed to answer. The guy hadn't gotten cuffed or anything, so he would have been able to go offline with no problem.

I wonder if I'll meet him again tomorrow, I thought.

"Also, he gave me this," said the guard and handed me a letter.

"Thank you." I opened it and instantly realized that it was a message he'd left for me.

"Dear Ray Starling. I leave this message to you just in case you choose to stay in this world and either return here safe and sound or your death penalty expires.

First of all, I would like to thank you. Without you, I couldn't have brought the children back to their parents or the lady we'd met in that alley.

You will likely be offered many rewards for acts such as defeating the Gouz-Maise Gang, and you can rest assured that it all belongs to you. I have no need for any of it. In fact, I'm incapable of taking any rewards from the kingdom's public institutions.

It hasn't been long since we've met, but I believe I have a good grasp of what kind of person you are. You will most likely hesitate to accept what you're offered. However, with you having been the only one capable of doing it, you *must* be the one to take the rewards.

Also, you can rest easy knowing that I have already received my prize. My rewards were lady Rebecca's smile and the tears of joy that she shed when I brought her little brother to her.

That was more than enough for me.

If you still feel apprehensive about it, you can pay me back by treating me to lunch the next time we meet.

Please excuse the fact that it's in written form, but this is my goodbye to you.

Farewell. I hope we meet again. *Au revoir. À bientôt.*

The machine knight of ice and roses, Hugo Lesseps."

I was speechless.

In case I choose to stay in this world, huh? I thought. *I...*

281

"Umm... Ray?" As I got lost in thought, Liliana looked at me with worry in her eyes.

"Are you sure you are feeling well?" she asked.

"Oh, sorry about that," I said. "I'm quite fine, thank you."

"Well, if you say so... Anyway, since you have defeated the Gouz-Maise Gang, please take some time within the next few days to report it to the Adventurers' Guild and the knight offices. The Adventurers' Guild is for the bounties, while the knights need to know about the elimination of a criminal organization."

"I see. Thank you."

"The day is getting late now, and I believe you are exhausted beyond belief, so please go have some well-deserved rest," she said.

"I really should," I agreed. "It's been a really long day, after all. What will *you* do, Liliana?"

"I will go back to protecting Her Highness."

"...Clearly, I'm not the only one here who deserves to be thanked for all their efforts."

"Oh, there's no need, eheheh..."

"All right, I will take my leave now," I said.

"Feel free to," she said. "Let us meet again."

With that, Liliana and I parted ways.

Still logged in, I went on to take a nap in one of Gideon's inns. Once I let myself fall on the bed, all the events of the day flashed through my mind. However, due to how exhausted I was, the sandman took me before I could think about any of it.

This time, I didn't have any dreams.

The next morning, I woke up surprisingly early.

There was no sunlight flowing through the window and the sky outside only looked mildly bright, so it was probably before dawn. I placed my hand on my head and instantly found that the dog ears that had tortured me throughout all of yesterday were gone. With me spending the night in-game, they'd likely gone away due to the time limit.

"Have you awoken, Ray?" a voice asked.

I looked to where I'd heard the voice — the side opposite to the window. There, I saw Nemesis, who was sitting in a chair and looking at me.

"Morning, Nemesis," I greeted her.

"Good morning, Ray," she responded.

After that, we both just wordlessly looked at one another.

Eventually, I broke the silence and invited Nemesis for a walk. I took her to the plains right beyond Gideon's northern gates. With it being my third time here, the area was already becoming familiar to me.

Nemesis and I were speeding through it while riding Silver. I held the reins and controlled the steed while Nemesis sat behind and held onto me by my waist.

"This is truly pleasant," said Nemesis.

"Sure is," I agreed.

As I had such meaningless exchanges with Nemesis, I continued making Silver gallop through the plains. After about thirty minutes had passed, I saw the sun begin to show itself from behind the eastern mountains.

"Will you leave this world?" That was when Nemesis asked me that question.

I said nothing. She was referring to what I had been considering back in the fortress' basement.

If I processed *Infinite Dendrogram* the same way I did reality, it was questionable whether staying in a world so filled with death would be a good thing for me. The sight of the corpses of children I didn't even know had been enough to make me feel as though my heart had been gouged out. If they were people I was familiar with, like Liliana or Milianne, it would probably hurt me as much as a loss of a friend in reality.

However...

"There's more to this world than just loss," I said.

If I hadn't started Infinite Dendrogram, *I would've never met the sisters, Rook, Marie, Hugo, Cyco and — of course — you, Nemesis. I simply couldn't have come to know any of them if I'd only stayed there, and Nemesis wouldn't even have been born.*

"You *are* aware that you might go through something painful again, no?" she said.

Of course I am, I thought. *You're completely right about that. Events like what we went through yesterday are probably a daily occurrence here. But still...*

"If something that would leave a bad taste in my mouth starts happening before me... I'll just stop it," I said.

This time, it had been all over by the time I'd gotten there. However, if I was ever in the right place at the right time, I would do everything I could to prevent such a tragedy. After all, the possibility leading to the desired future was there, as long as you didn't give up.

"I would give my all to grab hold of the possibility," I said.

"I see," Nemesis spoke from behind me. "I feel like you are shouldering far more than you should, but I cannot say that this is unlike you. Yes — you should fight to protect. And while you do that…"

Still behind me, Nemesis gently patted me on the head.

The softness of the hand made me turn around.

"…*I* will be the one protecting *you*."

Nemesis, covered in morning light, gave me the most gentle smile.

That expression made me face forward again and swing Silver's reins to make him canter ahead. For some reason, I had become bashful enough that I was unable to look at her face again. Still, I felt that I had to say something back to her.

"Thanks… Nemesis…" That was all that came out.

As she held onto me, I felt as though she smiled once again.

After that, neither of us said anything more.

Still on Silver's back, we dashed through the fields as we let that gentle morning of smiles embrace us.

The surroundings of the east gate of Gideon, the city of duels
Midnight.

The day when Ray had fought and prevailed against the Revenant Ox-Horse, Gouz-Maise, had reached its end.

The surroundings of the east gate of Gideon — which were completely devoid of people with the exception of the few guards on their night shifts — were suddenly intruded by the appearance of a pair of people emitting a faint light.

One of them was a man clad in a military uniform reminiscent of a pilot suit — Hugo Lesseps, High Pilot of the Dryfe Imperium. Next to him was his Embryo, Cocytus.

After the last event, Hugo had logged out to avoid further questioning from the kingdom, and had now logged back in again after waiting for the right time.

After logging in, the two of them quickly walked away from the gate, entered a small alleyway, and began waiting for something. Less than a minute passed until someone came.

It wasn't a drunkard or some hoodlum.

Instead, it was a person wearing a penguin suit.

It was the very same penguin that had appeared before Ray last morning, pronounced himself "Dr. Flamingo," and gotten rid of Ray's debuffs while also giving him a pair of dog ears.

"Kept ya waiting," said the penguin.

"Not at all," replied Hugo. "I spent most of the waiting time offline."

"You were pretty busy today, weren't ya? Took care of the gang that was troubling this town, eh?"

"You're aware?" Hugo asked.

"Indeed I am," said the penguin. "I was doing some wiretapping on Ray, you see."

"Wiretapping Ray? How?"

"Not telling. I've been listening on him like I would a radio drama, and boy, was it a good one. He's as much of a Maiden's Master as you are, Hugh." The penguin made his body sway and chuckled.

"Well, if you know what he was doing, there's something I'd like you to tell me…" said Hugo.

"Yep, he won," the penguin answered the question before it was even asked. "Victory is his. He actually solo'd a UBM."

"I see. That's good to know." Hugo wasn't lying when he said that. However, that sentiment was followed by thoughts that completely contradicted it.

If the UBM had given him the death penalty, we probably wouldn't have to face each other today. After all, a person so straightforward in nature will surely try to stop the plan. Wait, in the first place, should I really be taking an active part in a plan that Ray would try to stop?

Little by little, hesitation began to envelop Hugo's mind.

"So, Hugh, are you ready for tomorro— no, today's plan?" the penguin asked, as if it was fully aware of Hugo's inner struggle.

Hugo quickly held back the hesitation, and reported something. "The Marshall II was destroyed."

"I see," said the penguin. "Here's a Garage with a spare one, then. It's Marshall II Revised — an improved version of the Marshall II you were using before. Its defense and AGI are 30% higher. The fine-tuning is done, too."

The penguin reached into his inventory and took out a large, rolled up, metallic scroll much like the one Hugo had used in the afternoon.

"Thank you very much," Hugo said gratefully. "Oh, I just remembered this."

Hugo took out a bundle of papers from his inventory. It was the sorcery blueprint that he'd discovered in the hideout of the Gouz-Maise Gang.

"Oh yeah, the sorcery that created that UBM, eh?" said the penguin.

"Well, with the clan already having scrapped the grudge power plan, I think it's probably useless to us," Hugo commented.

"Well, you think right," said the penguin. "After all, we got help from the King of Tartarus for that one, so the sorcery of a high-rank tian is just a bit…"

"Leader?"

The penguin was looking down at the blueprint and silently examining the text. "I see… So just because it's grudge, it doesn't have to… This needs to be verified, though…"

After making some conclusions, the penguin put the blueprint into his inventory.

"Back to the matter at hand," he said. "With that Garage I gave you, you are prepared to be the heart of this plan. Other preparations are just about complete, as well."

The penguin began counting down his fingers to confirm what was done or not. Since the suit didn't have any fingers fit for counting, he obviously did it with the human fingers inside.

"The deployment of Castling and the gadgets is done. The arrangements to allow us to influence the device are done. The club, Veldorbell, has been taking root there for a few days now. And of course, my — the diamond's — preparations are done... or so I'd like to say. But there's something I still have to do. Well, it's not like I won't make it in time for the plan."

Adding the names of playing card suits here and there, the penguin shared info with Hugo.

Though it seemed like some sort of coding, it was far simpler than that. When creating plans, the penguin simply had a habit of giving the codenames based on card suits to those who had important roles.

"The only real cause of worry here is whether the imperator's joker is actually gonna do her job or not, but it all depends on luck," said the penguin. "Still, she'll probably act as long as our sources are correct and the first princess actually comes."

"Umm, what's this plan's spade?" Hugo realized that that suit hadn't been mentioned, and decided to ask about it.

That was because, whenever using suits as codenames, the penguin always gave spade to either the trump card or the most destructive role in his plan.

The penguin's answer was simple. "Ah, well... I don't have one. No spade this time."

It seemed as though he was hiding something, but Hugo didn't bother to doubt him.

"But man, am I glad. The event is actually happening." As if to change to subject, the penguin nodded and continued talking. "Seriously, I can't be more glad. I have no clue what retard was responsible for it, but the blockade caused by the PK happening almost ruined the event and our plan with it."

The PK happening. That was the event in which three player-killing clans and the Superior Killer had created a blockade in the four newbie hunting grounds around the capital. Though the kingdom's four Superiors had taken care of the problem, it had already affected the kingdom's overall power.

On the internet, it was rumored that it had been done by the imperium, which was on the verge of war with the kingdom. However, the penguin knew better than everyone that it wasn't true.

"Who do you think was responsible for that?" asked Hugo.

"No clue," curtly answered the penguin. "They went about it so well that they didn't leave any proof behind. Though the PKs were rewarded with pretty nice sums of money. And besides our country, there weren't many groups that relied on using coinage like that."

"Caldina, then?" asked Hugo.

Caldina, the commercial city-state union.

It was a mercantile country that covered the entire desert in the center of the continent and claimed that the presence or lack of money was everything.

Its national characteristic was that people there could get special products from all the other countries — albeit for large sums of money. Due to that, many high-end players had moved there, causing it to become the strongest country in terms of the amount of Masters.

"For what purpose did they do it?" asked Hugo.

"Well, I think there's more to it than just sullying the imperium's reputation," answered the penguin. "That place has both tians and Superiors that really know how to use their heads. They could have just used Sefirot — their pride and joy — yet instead they messed around with these indirect methods. What a pain."

Sefirot was the name of the top clan in the commercial city-state union of Caldina. Though it was only a mere ten members strong, a whole nine of them were Superiors.

Among those nine were The Earth AKA the "Magically Strongest," King of Termination AKA the "Seven Death Transformation," God Hunter AKA the "Multifariously Invincible," and Ace AKA the "Blue Sky Songstress," all of whom were famous for their battle prowess.

Because of that, Sefirot was considered to be the strongest clan in all of *Infinite Dendrogram*.

"What is the likelihood of Sefirot showing up while the plan is commencing?" asked Hugo.

"I'm pretty sure they're unaware of it," said the penguin. "After all, if the plan is successful, it's likely that the kingdom will give up before the war even happens. It's like the imperium's decisive blow. If they knew about it, they would've already done something."

After saying that, the penguin began to consider.

"However, there's a chance that one or few of them came to see the event… The Clash of Superiors. If that happens, I'll just have to wreck their shit with the spade."

The penguin's words made Hugo begin to ponder.

Upon seeing that, the penguin talked to him with a gentle tone. "No need to overthink it, Hugo. If this goes well, the war will end with only minimal casualties."

"Minimal?" asked Hugo.

"Indeed. His Excellency the General(lel) wants an all-out war, but that would be a waste of all kinds of resources. Such things are best handled in ways that are both smart and exciting." Saying that, the penguin removed his suit. At the same time, he reached into his inventory, took out a lab coat, and put it on.

The result was a lean, spectacled man clad in a lab coat. He extended his hands to the sides and made a sonorous declaration.

"Tomorrow, we — The Triangle of Wisdom — will put a decisive end to the war between the imperium and the kingdom."

To be continued next episode…

Bear: "Heyo! Time fur another afterword! (Been awhile since the last one.)"

Cat: "And so, volume 2 was able to come out without any probleems."

Bear: "This is all thanks to the readers who bought volume 1, the stores that sold it…"

Cat: "…the editors, and Taiki and all the wonderful illustrations he drew!"

Bear: "Now, you might be aware of this, but a lot has happened between the releases of volume 1 and volume 2."

Cat: "First, there was the great *Dendro* festival on Twitterr!"

Bear: "It had all this unbearably good *Dendro* art drawn by a whole fifty illustrators!"

Cat: "You can go and check it out in the gallery of the official *Dendro* siite!"

Bear: "Also, it was announced that *Dendro* is getting a manga adaptation."

Cat: "The one working on it is none other than Kami Imai of *Needless* faame."

Cat: "Though that still wasn't revealed at the time this afterword was written."

Cat: "However, when volume 2 comes out, the first chapter should already be ouut."

Bear: "It's highly recommended that readers of these novels get their paws on that!"

Cat: "Search for it on Comic Firee!"

Bear: "Now, a word from our author."

Hello, this is Sakon Kaidou.

First of all, I would like to thank you getting your hands on *Infinite Dendrogram* volume 2.

Because of everyone involved and the audience, volume 1 sold well and we were able to release volume 2 into the world without much trouble, and I couldn't be more grateful for that.

Now, as you might be aware, the first volume had some typos and mistakes (in the Japanese release) which — unlike with webnovel uploads — couldn't be fixed after they were done. That made me painfully aware of my own lack of experience.

Releasing books into the world and having an audience buy them involved a level of responsibility completely unlike that of a webnovel author. I will try to become familiar with it and continue publishing *Infinite Dendrogram* to the best of my ability.

With that settled, it's planned that in the upcoming volumes 3 and 4, you'll be presented with the climax of the first part of *Infinite Dendrogram*.

New characters, a great event in the city of duels, Superiors making their moves, and the first clash between Ray and a certain person who's been involved with him since the very beginning.

I would be a very happy author if you, the readers of volume 2, became reasonably excited for what's to come.

Thank you once again, and I hope this continues.

Sakon Kaidou

Cat: "…I suuure hope volume 2 doesn't have any typos."

Bear: "Well, according to head editor K, 'typos happen.'"

Cat: "And with that, it's time to end volume 2's afterwoord."

Bear: "It was brought to you by Brother Bear the bear…"

Cat: "…and Cheshire the caat!"

Bear: "Volume 3 is set to come out this year, so bear with us until then!"

Cat: "…It would be pretty surprising if it doesn't come out in 2017, right?"

Bear: "I-I'm sure it'll come out just fine."

Gamei Hitsuji
lustration=himesuz

The Magic in This Other World is Too Far Behind!
Volumes 1-4 Available Now!

In Another World With My Smartphone

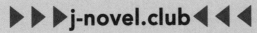

J-Novel Club Lineup

Ebook Releases Series List